A Bridgetender's View:

Notes on Gratitude

Barb Abelhauser

bridgetender, dog lover, daily blogger

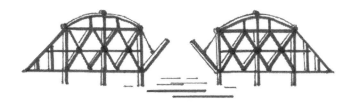

Collected stories from "The View from a Drawbridge:
The random musings of a bridgetender with
entirely too much time on her hands."

Barb Abelhauser
The View from a Drawbridge
PO Box 77052
Shoreline, WA 98177
babel@barbabelhauser.com

www.theviewfromadrawbridge.wordpress.com

www.theviewfromadrawbridge.com

ISBN-10: 1536981575
ISBN-13: 978-1536981575

DEDICATION

For my sister, Andrea McWilliams, my fierce defender, unwavering supporter, cat whisperer and baker of the world's best apple pies.

In memory of Chuck Guerra, who gave me so much to be grateful for.

CONTENTS

ACKNOWLEDGEMENTS

Given that this is an anthology on gratitude, it becomes all the more clear to me that I have a lot of people to be grateful for.

Without the support of Deborah Drake, my editor, my catalyst, my publicist, my consultant, my friend, and my unwavering source of encouragement, this book would not exist. Thanks also to Amy Sassenberg for her gorgeous photographs and for bringing beauty to my life in general, and to Bronte Polette for taking one of my favorite bridge photographs and working her magic to make a book cover image that makes me proud, as well as being a much-needed source of technical brilliance when it came to photo editing. Much gratitude to Vicky Cabe Autry for leaving her comfort zone and creating an illustration featured on the cover and throughout these pages that makes drawbridges look like angel wings, which is how I have viewed them all along. And much love to Amelia Isabel, for writing my foreword, and for being one of my most enthusiastic cheerleaders.

I also can't thank enough the loyal readers of my blog, The View from a Drawbridge; the many people who inspired me to write entries; and friends and family who have supported my efforts. If I've left anyone out below, I sincerely apologize.

First, those who defy easy alphabetization: My mom, Sonia, Tony, Seattle Park Lover, Paula Delles and Kevin Ross, Kramer, Calypso Castaignede and Morgaine McBride, Angiportus, Paulette, Dr. Elizabeth Joneschild and Dr. Stephen Markowitz, Martin Hunt and Elaine Lorefield

And last but not least, Linda and Paul Beiderwell, Tommie Benefield, Bailey Bennett, Martine Bernadel, Bill Bernat, Arthur Browne, Betty Buckland, Valarie Bunn, Aline Burchfield, Linda Cooke, Cailey Cron, Paul Currington, Gabby De Cicco, Stephanie Darnell, Ann Degnan, Raquel DeHoyos, Julie Dinsmore-Myers, Patricia Driscoll-Baden, Jennifer Dropkin, Max Fabella, Neal Fallen, Lynn Fitz-Hugh, Liz Stanford Fuller, Juan Carlos Garcia Romero, Harold George, Chuck Guerra, Arlo Guthrie, Jim Henson, Deborah Holihan, Ryan Hovendick, Leah Hurley, Ronnie and Donnie Hurt, Jim Jarman, Bob Johnson, Sean Kagalis, Helen and Colin Klett, Mary Kutheis, Vicki LaRue, Anju Lavina, Carole Lewis, Deb Martin, Albert McWilliams, Kathleen Mercier, Sarah Mercier, Daniel Joseph Murray, Diana Nyad, Pamela Pollock, Sam Ramirez, Florita Robinson, Frank Santana, Susan Schon, Wade P. Streeter, Lyn Sutton, Karen Swanepoel, Sandi Akins TenPas, Betti Thomasian, Raymond Tierney, Tracy Tinsley, Buz Wickless, and Areiel Wolanow.

~Barb Abelhauser

FOREWORD

By Amelia Isabel Torres

What makes a person extraordinary?

Many scenes come to mind of people doing death-defying feats and courageous acts of kindness. For me, it's when an ordinary human being can step in front of an audience, captivate them, and transport them into a whole new way of seeing the world.

The author of this anthology is one such person for me.

I first met Barb at a storytelling event in Seattle last fall. I went on a whim, wanting to brush up on my storytelling skills; and as a way to connect to the latest city I was checking out. I had been living nomadically and traveling through the western U.S. for the last five months. On this particular night, I was desperately craving interaction with other creative brains.

I perused Seattle's Meetup community and found Fresh Ground Stories. Their upcoming event listed "Comfort Zone" as the month's storytelling theme. How apropos, I thought, recalling all the recent times I slept on the side of mountain roads, rivers, waterfalls, gas stations, and Wal-Mart parking lots. I smiled and rsvp'd for the event later that night.

Being no stranger to Open Mic nights, I felt pretty confident in my abilities. I even took the theme literally and purposely did not prepare anything--to challenge my own comfort zone. The night of the event, I sauntered into Roy Street Coffee House at the north end of Broadway Avenue in Capitol Hill, placed my name on a yellow slip of paper and slipped it into the first timer's tin, and then found a seat. When emcee and meetup organizer, Paul Currington called my name, I walked coolly up to the mic, paused dramatically, and recited the first story that came to mind. The audience applauded when I finished, and I took my seat, satisfied with my performance. I settled into my chair, sat back and listened as the next storyteller took to the stage. With each new tale told, I laughed, I clapped, and I cried--fully content with my choice in having come.

Then, the next storyteller's name was called. A woman sporting a purple shirt, jeans, and an A-line salt and pepper bob hairstyle approached the mic. She adjusted her glasses and cleared her throat. The audience grew quiet. She stared at the floor for a moment, took a deep breath, then raised her head and began. She said her name was Barb and that she was a bridgetender, a person who opens and closes drawbridges for a living. My eyes widened. The thought never occurred to me that there was even a person sitting somewhere on the bridge manning it. Prior to this moment, I had assumed that drawbridges opened automatically by a sensor or something. She went on, detailing her daily routine which included watching boats float up and down the river, identifying the big ones that needed an opening, radioing the vessel to confirm they required an opening, pushing a button to turn the traffic lights to red, waiting for the traffic to clear, and checking to be sure no soul was crossing the bridge before she, by the power of her index finger, opened the drawbridge.

I was astounded. I leaned forward in my seat, hanging on her every word.

Barb continued. She revealed that she had been tending bridges for fourteen years, holding the second highest record for most drawbridges operated in a career. She had recently moved from Jacksonville, Florida, and recounted her experiences working the Ortega River Drawbridge. She explained how sitting in a lone booth up above a flowing river allows a person to essentially become a professional observer of the natural world. Barb is skilled in being exquisitely aware of the passing of time, the migration patterns of birds, and the perpetual sliding of the sun across the horizon year after year. She spoke endearingly of a reliable alligator popping his head out of the water in the same spot under her bridge every day like a living cuckoo clock. She recognized the different joggers and walkers who crossed the bridge daily, all completely oblivious that somewhere on that very bridge was an invisible tower with a hidden guardian tenderly keeping watch over them. "Best of all," she beamed, "executives in million dollar suites cannot buy a view better than mine."

By the end of her story, I had leaned so far forward in my seat that I could taste the shampoo of the person sitting in front of me. Who is this woman?? I thought. I HAVE to meet her! When she finished, she offered an open invite to anyone interested in a tour of her drawbridge, and I immediately was like: ME! I could barely contain my emotion by the time the event finished that I am fairly certain I bum-rushed her with a gigantic hug, showering her in an unintelligible gush of adulation and flattery. I don't think she quite knew what to do with all my enthusiasm, but she studied me and, seeming to have made up her mind that I was harmless, offered a friendly smile and thanks. I told her that I was interested in touring her bridge, and with a twinkle in her eye, she said, "Sure, okay."

We met the following week at the University Bridge in Seattle's University District. We walked along the pedestrian path with Barb proudly explaining the bridge's history, pointing out its key architectural components, and describing how the bascule or counterweight works to lift the bridge and open it in two. Barb offered anecdotes about how she often wonders who the first woman bridgetender was and what life might have been like for her or about how when she turns the traffic lights to red, she watches as harried motorists brake and peel away towards the back roads. She shook her head, "If only they knew it actually takes longer for them to go all the way around versus just sitting and waiting for four minutes for me to open and close the bridge." I imagined myself probably having sped away just like those impatient drivers. She also shared with me that in fourteen years of tending bridges and countless invitations to family and friends, she never once had given anyone a tour. I gaped at her, realizing that she probably spent the last decade and a half perfecting the perfect tour of her drawbridge, and I was the lucky recipient.

We slowed to pause in the middle of the bridge and gazed off into the horizon, content in each other's silent company. We watched as the sun slowly dipped below the expressway that hung in the vista across from her bridge. I smiled and sent a quiet prayer of gratitude to the universe for having aligned us to meet. Barb spoke then, reflecting on our afternoon, and said, "I can't help but think that your perspective has changed now; that every time you cross a drawbridge from here on out, you'll always remember this experience." I smiled then, and I am smiling now because she was right. Not only because of my newfound appreciation of drawbridges but because of Barb. She gave me a new way of seeing the world. It's because of her encouragement that I started my podcast series, Shaping Sapiens, and I was pleased when she agreed to be featured as my first story and guest.

Barb Abelhauser--who loves her job as a bridgetender-- reminded me that if I just stop more often and open my eyes to my surroundings, the extraordinary can be found in the ordinary--in the invisible.

And for that, I am eternally grateful.

~Amelia Isabel Torres, **Shaping Sapiens**
podcaster/writer/community-builder

INTRODUCTION

I have been opening drawbridges for a living since 2001. Most of the time it's a kind of Zen-like existence. The isolation appeals to me. I feel as though this job has given me the gift of time. Time to think. Time to observe the world. Time to be inspired so I could rush home and write.

I began my daily blog, The View from a Drawbridge, in December of 2012. I assumed it would last for about 6 months and then I'd run out of things to say. It had no fixed theme. I call it "The random musings of a bridgetender with entirely too much time on her hands."

But then in April, 2013, I heard a radio interview with David George Haskell, a biologist who spent a year studying just one square meter of old growth forest in Tennessee. By observing that one patch of ground from one fixed point, he was able to learn a lot of amazing things. After hearing that, it suddenly occurred to me that my blog has a theme after all! All my entries have to do with my minute observations from my drawbridge.

Most people don't even realize I'm up in my tower, but oh, I see them. I also see nature as it changes from season to season, and patterns that the casual observer would most likely miss. These are the observations that inspire my blog entries.

I could easily have contented myself with quietly blogging away, but then a whole series of amazing things happened. I discuss those things in more detail in "My Latest Story—Wrong Can Be Right" and "On Being Busy" here in this anthology. The main thing to know is that I was contacted by StoryCorps and asked if I'd be willing to have an interview that I did for them back in 2009, published in their book *Callings: The Purpose and Passion of Work* by Dave Isay.

The interview was about how much I love being a bridgetender. (Incidentally, I'm no longer doing it for lousy pay and benefits as I once was. Much was made of that statement, but it's a thing of the past.) This topic got me a great deal more attention than I anticipated, and the result is this anthology. That phone call was the catalyst that sent me careening off into the world of publishing.

Each book in this series will have a theme, something I've written about on many occasions in my blog. It seemed appropriate to start off with the subject of gratitude, since I'm so grateful to be where I am now, surrounded by the amazing people in my life.

And I will be donating 10 percent of the profits from each book to a nonprofit organization. It is only fitting that in this instance my first choice would be StoryCorps.

So I hope you enjoy my random musings on gratitude, and encourage you to visit http://theviewfromadrawbridge.com and subscribe to my blog--which pairs well with a morning cup of tea or coffee, according to a good friend of mine.

Keep in touch!

~Barb Abelhauser

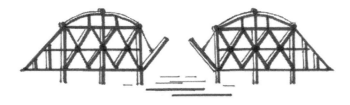

Gratitude

*Sometimes your gratitude is all about the pure joy
of having things to be grateful for!*

Ever since I moved to Seattle, I've sort of felt as if my heart has come to reside outside of my ribcage. Vulnerable. Exposed. Sensitive. It's kind of a crazy feeling. I need to develop a thicker skin.

I've just been through so much in the past couple years. I've given up so much, sacrificed so much. I've taken some insane risks, some of which have paid off, and some of which have blown up in my face.

But on a positive note, this has caused me to appreciate all the good in life so much more deeply. When I think of my friends and loved ones, near and far and old and new, I often well up with tears of joy. A good sunrise can take my breath away. I can be walking down the street and suddenly it hits me how lucky I am to be where I am, and I have to stop dead in my tracks for a second and gather myself.

In essence, I've become a sentimental old fool. And I wouldn't have it any other way.

First published on <u>*November 29, 2015*</u>

Awe

*This entry kind of puts all this gratitude in perspective,
and it never fails to cheer me up!*

awe
[aw]
noun
1. an overwhelming feeling of reverence, admiration, fear, etc.,
produced by that which is grand, sublime, extremely powerful,
or the like.

Dear readers, I have to say that it is truly wonderful to be a
human being. For many reasons. Not the least of which is our
ability to be self-aware. Even now, you can easily imagine
looking down at yourself as you read this. Other animals can't
do this. That's why cats and dogs get so confused by mirrors.
They have no concept of themselves as separate entities.

What a gift this is! Because of this self-awareness, we are able
to be very aware of others as well. We can be in awe. We can
appreciate skill and kindness and talent and compassion. We
can try to be better people based on what we see as valuable
qualities in those we admire.

I absolutely love to be in awe of other people, because it means
I'm open to possibilities. It means that it isn't over for me.
There's always something to strive for, something to aspire to.

And if, like me, you believe in the interconnectedness of all
things, then being in awe is even more priceless, because it

means that there are things in this wholeness of which we are a part that are pure and good and wonderful to behold. I don't know about you, but that makes me feel really good about me, and about all of us.

Just something to think about during your next traffic jam.

First published on <u>December 1, 2015</u>

"It's a Ride Naked on a Tricycle Kind of Day"

When I wrote this entry back in 2013 I was still rather stiff and self-conscious. Since then, thanks to the freewheeling city in which I now live and the wonderful friends I've made, I'm much more relaxed, and oh, so much happier!

A friend of mine sent out a picture of his toddler doing just that the other day, and that was the caption below it. I thought, "I have those kinds of days, but only in my head."

That reminded me of one of my pet peeves. Why do children get to do things that adults would never dare to do? I want to jump in puddles! I want to make mud pies! I want to go down a slip n' slide! I want to blow bubbles in my milk! I want to have a tree house!

My mother used to adore merry-go-rounds. I still have an image of her in my head, riding on one in her early 40's, sitting stiffly upright but looking absolutely delighted. At the time I was so young that I didn't realize how special that was. It takes a lot for an adult to do something like that. Why is that?

Some people have children or grandchildren and can use them as an excuse to let their inner child come out to play. But for those of us who have no children, or whose children have all grown up, I feel it's important to remind oneself to remain playful. When I see a couple that is playful with each other, I always think, "I want to have a relationship, heck, I want to have a *life* like that."

Somewhere along the line most of us become more reserved. It sneaks up on us gradually. One day we look up and realize we're no longer someone who gets into snowball fights or does a Chinese Fire Drill at stoplights. And that is most definitely our loss.

In college at the dances, a friend of mine used to link hands with me and we'd spin in circles. It was so liberating! Just 3 or 4 short years later I visited her on campus. She now worked there. We happened to find ourselves at a dance and I wanted to spin, for old time's sake. She wouldn't, or couldn't, do it. As a staff member, she had an image to uphold. That made me profoundly sad.

But we don't have to walk that path if we don't want to. We can still be responsible adults while tossing the occasional water balloon. So your assignment, should you choose to accept it, is to find yourself a puddle and jump in it. I won't tell.

First published on July 25, 2013

"Ja, das ist der Platz"

Dogs definitely know how to appreciate the little things. We could all learn from them.

Standing in line on a dock in Croatia, waiting for the hydrofoil to Venice, I noticed a German tourist with her dog in tow. I hadn't seen my dogs in weeks and missed them terribly. Using hand signals to break the language barrier, I asked if I could pet her dog. She nodded.

I began scratching his back, and he gave that shudder of pure ecstasy so typical of canines when you hit that sweet spot. You know the one. It made me smile. And the lady said, "Ja, das ist der Platz." Even though I don't speak German, I knew exactly what she meant. Yes, that's the place. That phrase trips through my mind now whenever I pet my own dogs.

How wonderful it must be to have something so simple and innocent transport you to nirvana. I want a platz! (And yeah, I know what you're thinking. Shame on you. But that's not what I mean.)

First published on <u>August 9, 2013</u>

"You Deserve to be Happy."

If you always remember to be grateful for the good that comes into your life, rather than becoming resentful of what you think you deserve but don't have, contentment will be yours.

I saw that tag line in a Facebook advertisement for therapy, and it made me think of a conversation I had with a friend from Burma. He said, "In the West, you think you deserve happiness, so you get upset, depressed, anxious or bitter if you don't have it. In the East, we don't expect happiness, so we're delighted when it comes our way."

Like many things, it's all a matter of perspective. And it is a good question. *Why* do we think we deserve to be happy? What makes us so special? Do we think we were born with some sort of golden ticket? "Happiness, Admit One."

It's natural to strive for happiness. But it might be healthier to look at it as a gift rather than a right. That way, when you don't have it, you don't feel like it's some sort of failure on your part, and when you do have it, you'll feel like you've won a prize, and can appreciate it all the more.

First published on April 21, 2015

"You're never too old to live your dreams."

*I will remain forever grateful for those who have gone
before me who serve as incredible role models.
Diana Nyad is definitely one of those.*

Thank you, Diana Nyad, for reminding us all of this when you swam for about 53 hours from Cuba to Florida at the age of 64.

This amazing feat reminded me of the many other people I have heard of who have done incredible things at an advanced age.

Mother Teresa won the Nobel Peace Prize at the age of 69.

Mavis Lindgren ran her first marathon at age 70.

An ex-boyfriend's 80-year-old mother recently went white water rafting down the Colorado River.

At age 61, and weighing only 99 pounds, Gandhi walked almost 200 miles to protest the British salt tax.

As a Learn to Read volunteer, I have encountered many seniors who have chosen to learn to read for the first time in their lives.

Grandma Moses, the renowned American folk artist, did not begin to paint seriously until she was 76. One of her paintings eventually sold for 1.2 million dollars.

Reverend Scott Alexander, who lead the church I used to attend, rode his bike 3,300 miles across the country last summer to raise $50,000 and raise awareness about hunger. He is 63 years old.

Colonel Sanders was 66 when he started Kentucky Fried Chicken.

Nelson Mandela became president of South Africa when he was 76, and that's after suffering in prison for 26 years of his life.

Laura Ingalls Wilder, of "Little House on the Prairie" fame, did not publish her first book until she was 64, and continued to do so until she was 76.

So when Diana Nyad walked out of the ocean on shaky legs, sunburned, exhausted, and with her mouth full of sores from the salt water, and said, "You're never too old to live your dreams," she wasn't kidding. And to make it even more amazing, she had tried, and failed, 4 times before.

Never give up. If there's something you want to do, like travel or learn or create, don't let your age stand in your way. Use Diana Nyad's mantra: Find a way.

First published on <u>September 7, 2013</u>

A Different Breed of Ladies' Man

It's a pure delight to have friends who are nothing like you.
The contrasts leave room for learning.

The other night I had dinner with a friend who was just passing through. His work takes him all over the country. He fascinates me because we couldn't be more different. But in a good way.

I have to admit that normally extroverts get on my nerves. But his is a pure, clean, distilled form of extroversion. He's not attention seeking. He's not aggressive or loud. He's not in your face. He just genuinely and truly likes people. He likes meeting them, talking to them, interacting with them. Especially women. He has this affinity for women.

I'm not quite sure how he manages it, but he's drawn to women without any perverted intent whatsoever. He genuinely seems to respect them and isn't trying to get anything from them. He's not on the hunt. He doesn't have an agenda. It's refreshing.

At dinner he made it a point to learn the name of the waitress, and whenever she stopped by to check on us, he included her in our conversation and asked her opinion. As the restaurant was crowded, we sat at the bar. Throughout the night he'd also turn and chat to the much older lady sitting next to us. He helped her get ketchup out of the bottle. He recommended the smoked sea salt. The cherries with our salmon were so delicious that he said to her, "You've got to try this," and put a cherry on her plate. I was charmed. By the end of the night he knew where she was from and what she was doing here.

Whenever I get the opportunity to spend time with this man, I'm reminded of how completely different we are, and I just kind of sit back and watch, thinking, "This is a rare creature, indeed." I will always appreciate the fact that he's on the planet, roaming free, and look forward to future opportunities to interact with him in his natural habitat. Because it's a delightful, friendly place indeed.

First published on February 13, 2015

A Floridian Gets Snowed Upon

*After not having seen snow in decades, I was able to take a
moment to really enjoy nature's transformation.
And then I had to drive in it. I'm really glad
I have a better car than I did when I wrote this!*

I woke up one recent winter morning to discover that the
world was covered in a white powdery substance that I hadn't
seen in 30 years. It instantly transported me back to my
childhood in Connecticut. I wanted to turn on the radio to see if
my school was having a snow day.

We moved to Florida when I was 10 years old, so all my
memories of snow are delightful ones. I played in it. I didn't
have to shovel it or drive in it or worry about the heating bill or
frozen pipes. My mother would spend 20 minutes bundling me
into my snow suit so I'd look like the Michelin Tire Man, and I'd
go play for 15 minutes and then want to come back inside, and
I'd expect a hot drink to be waiting for me. (I'm amazed I
survived to adulthood.) And in college in North Carolina we'd
steal trays from the cafeteria and go sledding, and have epic
snowball fights.

So here I was, all grown up and looking at this transmuted
snowy landscape and I immediately got excited. I took pictures.
I let my dogs out. They'd never seen snow in their lives.

Devo took it in stride. Blue, on the other hand, is a bit high
maintenance. He doesn't like to get his feet wet. So he stood on

the back stoop and barked at it indignantly, then came inside and pooped on the living room carpet.

After cleaning up after my dumb dog, it suddenly occurred to me that I was going to have to drive in this stuff. I still had to go to work. And I've never driven in snow in my life. I got lucky, though. Most of it had already melted off the pavement. Still, I took it extremely slowly. I managed to make it to work without killing myself or anybody else, but it was a miracle because my defroster doesn't work and there was ice on the inside of my windshield. And when I left work to come home, my door lock was frozen and I had to climb in from the passenger side.

It wasn't pretty, but I got the job done. It's all part of adjusting to my new life. I kind of like the idea that every once in a while, I will look out the window and what I will see will be transformed.

What a concept.

First published on <u>December 3, 2014</u>

A New Point of View

Pushing yourself out of your comfort zone can be exciting and revitalizing. I highly recommend it.

Every once in a while, it's fun to shake things up. Sticking to a routine may feel quite comfortable, but it isn't particularly exciting. So recently I volunteered to trade bridges with a coworker, just for a day. I got to work at Fremont Bridge here in Seattle.

It's been well over a year since I set foot on this bridge. I actually had to stare at the operating console for a while and read the instructions to familiarize myself with the operation. No two drawbridges are quite the same. Each one has its quirks and blind spots and operating weaknesses, and the various nobs and switches and buttons are in different locations.

When I had my first opening of the day, I felt like a baby deer just learning to walk. But I did it! It's been quite some time since I've felt such accomplishment just by doing my job.

It's also given me a fresh perspective on this blog. As eclectic as it is, the overarching theme is that I get to examine the same view day after day, in minute detail. It allows me plenty of time to think about things and share those thoughts with you.

So all of a sudden, having a different view is a bit unsettling. Will I still be inspired? Will I be too distracted? Too nervous?

It does sort of feel as if I'm using a whole new set of synapses. I feel both revitalized and a little befuddled. I didn't realize how often I let myself go into "automatic pilot". I can't do that here. Nothing on this bridge is automatic for me. I miss my comfort zone, but at the same time this feels good for me. I think I'm going to have to make a mental note to do this every few months. Variety is, after all, the spice of life!

First published on May 9, 2016

My Latest Story--Wrong Can Be Right

Sometimes when things are beyond your control,
it's the best thing that can ever happen to you.
This story explains why this anthology exists.

I went to my monthly storytelling event while still in a delighted daze about all the amazing things that have been going on in my life, in terms of the StoryCorps anthology and the anthologies that I'm planning to publish myself, so naturally that's what I wanted to talk about, even though tooting my own horn does not come naturally to me.

But it was a tricky month for horn tooting, because the theme for this month's event was "Mistakes–Stories of Getting it Wrong." So I had to be a little creative.

Let me know how you think I did. Here's the recording of my story on Sound Cloud, and if you are unable to get audio or don't want to hear the dulcet tones of my voice, below that I'll post the text I practiced with for weeks prior to the event. I think I stayed pretty faithful to it this time.

https://soundcloud.com/theviewfromadrawbridge

I truly believe that if there's a lesson you're supposed to be learning but you aren't, then the universe will throw it at you over and over and over again until it finally sinks in. One of those lessons, for me, seems to be that despite my best efforts, life just isn't going to be predictable.

I'm a Capricorn through and through. I like everything to be foreseeable and expected. I like all my triangles to be equilateral and my t's to be crossed and my I's dotted. And my ducks better behave themselves and stay in a nice little row.

But if they don't, what will I do? What can I do? Nothing. Because life just isn't going to be predictable. I don't know why that always takes me by surprise. I think my life has taken an unusually high number of 90 degree turns simply because I'm supposed to be learning that lesson.

"You think you can have it all under control? Well, buckle up baby. Here we come!"

I have to say, though, that recently I've been enjoying this lesson a heck of a lot. It started when I got a phone call from StoryCorps asking if I remembered that interview I did for them back in 2009 about how much I loved being a bridgetender.

"Yes..."

"Well, we want to include it in our next book."

So there I am now, on page 17. They even spelled my name right!

But oh, that's not all. Of course they want to promote this book, so they asked if it would be all right if they played part of my interview on National Public Radio's Morning edition.
Heck yeah!

So now you can hear it on the NPR Website and the StoryCorps website. And because of that, overnight, visitors to my daily blog, the View from a Drawbridge, tripled in number.

Hooooo... so now things will die down and become nice and predictable again, right?

Noooooooo! Next, I was featured in Parade Magazine, which has a readership of 54 million.

And then a friend went to one of the book signings in Austin, Texas, and of the 53 people in this book, Dave Isay, the founder of StoryCorps, mentions my story specifically. What???

So now, when I Google my name, I get almost 4,000 results.

Even so, I wasn't expecting the next phone call, from a senior editor of O Magazine. Yup. I'm going to be in the September issue. Are you freakin' KIDDING ME? Oprah Winfrey is going to know my name for about two seconds! How cool is that?

I cannot believe this is happening to me. I'm so excited! I'll ride this wave as long as I can, even though sometimes it can be a little bit exhausting.

But I'm now working with the AMAZING Deborah Drake to start publishing a series of anthologies based on my blog.

Predictable life? Pfft. Little did I know.

First published on June 3, 2016

A Night Out with Friends-

In retrospect I'm rather proud of myself for my attitude, here. Rather than feeling sorry for myself for what I don't have, I chose to be encouraged that what I want is out there somewhere.

The other night I met a friend at Seattle's Royal Room to hear Leah Tussing, an amazing blues/jazz singer. She and her band were wonderfully talented and it was a very lovely way to spend a rainy, blustery evening.

The Royal Room itself is a comfortable, welcoming venue with good food and a relaxed atmosphere, but it was the company that made the event great. I also got to meet some new friends and that's always a pleasure.

All evening I got to watch my friend and her boyfriend interact, and it reaffirmed my faith that love can be magical. The way he looks at her, like she's the most wonderful, amazing person on the planet, gave me hope that someone would look at me that way again someday. I miss it.

She also hasn't been in the best of health this month, and he's been taking amazing care of her. That feeling of being with someone who has my back like that is another thing I long for. I was beginning to think it was a figment of my imagination.

And the affectionate touches? I will never EVER take a touch for granted again, as long as I live. A touch can mean everything. You don't realize it until you've lost it. Believe me.

Do I sound like I am feeling sorry for myself? On the contrary. That evening gave me hope. I left there feeling all warm and fuzzy, and very happy for my friend. Now I'm looking forward to what the future has in store for me. Anything is possible.

https://www.reverbnation.com/leahtussing
http://theroyalroomseattle.com/

First published on December 10, 2015

A Real Cliffhanger

This is one of my favorite blog entries because not only does it remind me of an amazing trip, but it also allows me to peek through the door into another world.

Back in 2005, I took a trip out west with my boyfriend at the time to Canyon De Chelly because I had a fascination with all things Anasazi. The canyon is now a national monument, but people have been living there for almost 5,000 years. Currently about 40 Navajo families are in residence. As with most of the rest of Arizona, the landscape is stunning.

To go into the canyon itself you need to take a tour or get a permit. We opted to go horseback riding with a Navajo guide. Frankly, I don't know how anyone manages to live there, because it is, in essence, a big bowl of sand. If not for the horses, we'd have been slogging along in calf high sand the vast majority of the time, with only the occasional grove of olive trees for shade, and no water to speak of.

Our guide took us to see some beautiful petroglyphs, and then, further along, some ancient cliff dwellings high above the canyon floor. I asked him if he had ever climbed up there, and he said, "No, because it would affect our bodies."

I thought that was a curious response, and it had me reflecting upon the great cultural divide between me and this man, who had not spoken much at all up to this point. He began to interest me more than the landscape we were travelling through. I'd ask him questions. He'd pause, as if considering the best way to dole out his words in the most economical fashion. Then he'd respond.

"Have you always lived in this area?" Pause. "Yes. Always."

Hours later, after his occasional brief response to my inquiries, for some reason the dam seemed to break. When I asked him if he'd ever been outside of this area he paused for a long time. Then he told me the following story.

"One time these people came here and booked a 3-day tour. The lady liked one of our horses so much that she offered to buy it, but she wanted us to deliver it to her home near Boston. So we did. We drove the whole way without stopping. Through many lands. Then we saw Boston."

"Did you get to see the ocean?"
"Yes."
"What did you think?"
"It was very big."

I will always have a mental image of this man gazing out at the Atlantic as if he had just arrived from another planet. "Then we came home."

At the end of the tour we said our goodbyes and I realized that this man had a much greater impact on me than I had on him. To him, I'm sure, I was like a brief wind. I wasn't the first. I wouldn't be the last. But to me, he was like a stone monument. He would always be there in my mind.

That night we camped, and the next day we drove along the rim of the canyon, stopping at each of the overlooks to take in the stunning views. I thought of him down there, my stone monument, doing his thing and living his life. He's part of that landscape for me now.

At the last overlook, the eerie western silence was broken by a strange sound. I couldn't identify it, and the first time I heard it, I thought it must have been my imagination. Then there it was again.

"Did you hear that?"
"No. What?"
"That!"

I got down on my hands and knees, and stuck my head over the side of the cliff, and sure enough, on a ledge about 3 feet below us was a skinny little puppy. He was shivering and crying.

"Oh, shit. We can't just leave it."
"Barb, it's a 1,000 foot drop."
"I know. But if I drive away and leave that dog, I'll never be able to live with myself."

And before he could say anything, I lowered myself down to the ledge, which, thank God, supported my weight. Don't look down, don't look down, don't look down...I grabbed the puppy, handed it to my boyfriend, climbed back up and walked as far away from the rim as I could get so as not to have the panic attack that I could feel trying to overtake me.

Alrighty then. Next. Feed the puppy. (And man, he was hungry. He ate half our picnic lunch.) I would have loved to keep him, but Florida was a long way away. So we took him to the ranger station, and they told us they'd bring him to a no kill shelter at the nearest town. We had one request.

"Tell them his name is Cliff."

First published on January 28, 2013

A Thousand Origami Cranes

*When feeling helpless, I am always grateful for something
to keep me busy that puts out positive energy.*

Many years ago I helped a friend fold a <u>thousand origami
cranes</u> for someone who had a brain tumor. I've always found
the Japanese legend of the thousand origami cranes to be
delightful. Some say that they will bring you good luck, or a
long life, or restored health.

Most believe that you must fold them yourself, and complete
them within one year, but I often see people making them for
others. Fathers will give them as a wedding gift to their
children, or they can be given to a baby for long life and good
luck. They are also given to certain temples as a prayer for
peace.

What I enjoy most about this tradition is that it's sort of the
physical manifestation of a prayer. I'm not one who prays. The
only time I even think about doing so is when I feel helpless.
Either I'm in a bad situation or someone I love is. Then I think
about praying, but am fairly confident that it won't do any
good. So, when feeling helpless like that, it would be
comforting to be doing something.

It would be good to at least live for a while in the illusion that I
have some control. Folding cranes will do nicely.

Also, I do believe that it never hurts to make your positive
desires visible to those around you. Saying that you wish

someone well is a wonderful thing to do, but origami cranes last longer, take more effort and therefore demonstrate your sincerity. And hey, they're pretty.

First published on <u>March 18, 2016</u>

A Vote from the Blue

*Since I wrote this entry, the coworker in question has
become one of the ones I respect and admire most.
Never take the good people in your life for granted!*

Have you ever felt like you've sunk to the very bottom of a
scummy pond and are looking up through the dirty yellow
water at a very weak and distant sun? Or perhaps you've been
fed through an emotional wood chipper? Good times. Good
times.

I had been weathering an emotional shit-storm not of my own
making for several days, and I was feeling pretty low.
Discouraged. Emotionally drained. I was second-, third-,
fourth-, and fifth-guessing myself. The rumor mill at work was
running at full tilt, and some of it was not particularly
complimentary.

At times like that, the most delicious feeling on earth is when
someone unexpectedly throws you a lifeline; a vote of
confidence, out of the blue. I arrived at work, disastrously un-
caffeinated and dreading another day of tumult, when the
phone rang. What now?

On the other end of that much-needed line was a coworker.
Our schedules are such that our paths almost never cross. I
may have spoken to him a total of 15 minutes in my entire life.
But he told me I was a good woman and a good employee and I
shouldn't let things get to me. He told me what it was like when

he started work many years ago as the only minority in a good ol' boys' club, and how hard that was.

I'm not sure I made it clear to him just how much that conversation meant to me. He gave me the strength to weather the storm. I'll be forever grateful for that small act of kindness.

Never underestimate how important your words of encouragement are to others. They may seem routine and obvious to you, but you could very well be delivering them as someone is about to hit rock bottom. That act may cost you nothing, but it might be priceless to the other person. That's a lovely return on an emotional investment!

First published on May 31, 2015

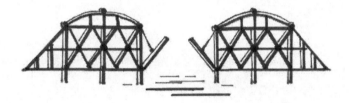

An Absence of Wrong Things

This entry was inspired by a long lost friend
who brought a great deal of wisdom into my life.
I'll be forever grateful for the memories.

I've discovered that it's never a good idea to try to solve the world's problems, or even my own, when I'm tired. Or hungry. Or lonely. Or angry. Or scared.

I was pretty much all of the above the other day, and I had a moment (a few hours, actually) of existential panic. I messaged a friend, "Am I doing the right thing?" He responded, "Do you see an absence of wrong things?"

What a wise and wonderful friend is he. Making this major change in location, job, and existence in general *has* deleted a lot of negative things from my life.

Cockroaches.
A job that did not pay me enough to survive.
Brutal heat.
A city that I've tried to get out of for thirty years.
Lots and lots and *lots* of ghosts.

Change is scary as hell, and I now have a mountain of debt to climb and a ton of challenges, and I'm all alone, and that is bound to freak me out now and then.

But maybe when I panic I just need to get a good night's rest, and then wake up and look at all the detritus I've left behind, and appreciate the fact that my life has become all that much lighter for having done so.

Wishing you an absence of wrong things!

First published on <u>*September 3, 2014*</u>

An Avalanche of Inspiration

When life hands you abundance, simply say,
"Thank you! More, please!"

Writing a daily blog for years on end can be a challenge. Sometimes I really struggle for a topic. I've even been known to post things on Facebook that say, "Help! I can't think of anything to write about in my blog!" So far I've always managed to come up with something, but a few times it was a very near thing indeed.

And then there are times like these. Times of abundance. I'm flush with a bountiful harvest of ideas. I have to make lists of things so as not to forget them. As we used to say in the South, I am in high cotton. I am looking at a few weeks where I won't have to sweat at all.

Why is this time different than others? That's my one source of frustration at the moment. I don't have a clue. Perhaps my muse just got back from the Bahamas or something. She's well rested, nicely tanned, and ready to get back to work. If there were some magic button to press to keep this momentum going, I'd be hopping up and down on it. As it stands, there just seem to be moments of feast and moments of famine.

The blog as a metaphor for life. I'll take it.

First published on February 12, 2016

An Ode to Counselors

I will always be grateful to those people in the helping professions. They are the ones who make it possible for the rest of us to live healthy and fulfilling lives.

I have a friend who is a Licensed Clinical Social Worker and she has a successful counseling practice. I can't imagine a more satisfying job. You're helping people cope who are carrying heavy emotional burdens. You are, essentially, lightening their load. How amazing. What a gift.

It sort of reminds me of the story of <u>Sisyphus.</u> He is doomed to push a heavy rock up a hill, only to have it roll back down again, causing him to start back over.

That, to me, is sort of what people who need counseling are like.

(Granted, Sisyphus was punished in this way for his deceitfulness and deserved what he got, but hey, don't mess with my analogy, here.)

People try so hard.
They heft that weight.
They shoulder that load.
But until they deal with it, they'll be rolling that rock forever.

My friend may not be able to take that rock away, but she can teach you how to balance it. That is a most valuable skill indeed, and it produces such positive results. But those outcomes are intangible to the outside world, so they must be easily overlooked.

So I wanted to take this opportunity to speak for the many people that she has helped over the years, and extend my appreciation to all the counselors out there:

Thank you.

First published on <u>May 28, 2015</u>

Anagnorisis and Peripeteia

Sometimes you can only appreciate an experience with benefit of hindsight. Those lessons can often be all the more precious for being hard-won.

I suspect that very few people outside of those who are serious literary scholars are familiar with these two terms, but we all should be, because most of us have experienced them at some point, and when we do, our lives change forever.

Let's start with definitions courtesy of dictionary.reference.com:

anagnorisis
[an-ag-**nawr**–*uh*-sis, –**nohr**-]

noun, plural **anagnorises**
(in ancient Greek tragedy) the critica lmoment of recognition or discovery, especially preceding peripeteia.

peripeteia
[per-*uh*-pi-**tahy**–*uh*, –**tee**–*uh*]

noun
a sudden turn of events or an unexpected reversal, especially in a literary work.

So, to oversimplify things, anagnorisis is that moment when the scales fall from your eyes and you realize something for the first time. As a New England friend of mine likes to say, "Dawn breaks on Marblehead." And that "whoa "moment, that anagnorisis, is what often throws you headlong into peripeteia, a turning point in your life.

Here are some examples:

Anagnorisis: Holy cow! I have the winning lottery ticket!
Peripeteia: Take this job and shove it!

Anagnorisis: My husband just allowed his boss to steal my life savings and has absolutely no intention of doing anything about it.
Peripeteia: Kindly sign these divorce papers. Now.

Anagnorisis: Being told the love of your life has died unexpectedly.
Peripeteia: Quitting your job and moving 3100 miles away to start your life over.

You might think of anagnorisis and peripeteia as the cruel handmaidens of fate, but often when you look back upon your meeting with them after the blessed passage of time, you will discover that they can be the best things that have ever happened to you. You never know when you'll cross paths with them, but speaking from experience, I owe them a debt of gratitude, and will make an effort to embrace them from now on when we cross paths. But I'll ask them politely to keep their visit brief, because their company, frankly, can be a bit draining.

First published on <u>May 5, 2015</u>

Applying for Friendship

If you want or need something in life, speak up!
You'll be glad you did.

I was sitting in a crowded little theater, waiting for a friend to do his one-man show, and I was chatting with another friend.

Someone asked us how we met, and my friend said, "She was advertising for friends, so I applied."

It's true.

During my first storytelling experience, in front of a crowd of 150 people, I explained what brought me to Seattle, and at the end I mentioned that with my weird work schedule, I had yet to make many friends here, so if anyone had room in their heart for me, there I was.

Afterward she came up to me and said, "I'll be your friend." And she has been, ever since. A lot of really fun experiences with her would never have happened if I hadn't spoken up.

How lucky am I?

Sometimes, even if you think it should be blatantly obvious, you just have to put your intentions or desires right out there for all the world to see. "I'm looking for friends." "I want to be in a relationship." "I *vont* to be alone." "I need help." Whatever it is that you want, need, or plan to do, spread the word.

People cannot read your mind. I sincerely believe that the majority of misunderstandings stem from the fact that we often forget that simple point. We are so used to hearing the thoughts inside our heads that on some level we overlook that no one else can.

So my advice for the day is, SPEAK UP!!!

First published on November 16, 2015

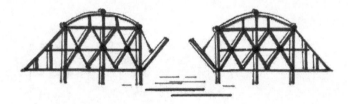

Champagne Relationships-

*The age-old struggle: is it better to have intimacy or
independence? I'm glad that in this modern age,
it is possible to have both. Even though
I've yet to find it myself, I still live in hope.*

One of my all-time favorite quotes is by Katharine Hepburn. "Sometimes I wonder if men and women really suit each other. Perhaps they should live next door and just visit now and then." That, to me, makes perfect sense.

Don't get me wrong. I absolutely love men, and miss having one in my life. But the older I get, the less willing I am to put up with things like sweaty socks in the coffee mug and extended debates over which direction the toilet paper should hang. I like having my own space and making my own decisions and having my own life.

Still, it would be nice to have a steady date on national holidays. And someone to go out to dinner with. And someone to call to talk me down off the ceiling when something has given me the creeps. And let's not forget the occasional, shall we say, biological gratification?

I was talking to a friend the other day, and she introduced me to the concept of Champagne Relationships. Someone you spend quality time with, and yet maintain a healthy amount of space from. All the bubble and the feeling of special occasions without any of the grit and sediment you get with home brew. All the sparkle without any of the polishing. No arguments over bathroom counter space. Separate living quarters, and your dust bunnies are none of my business or responsibility. An extended sense of newness and butterflies without any of the, "Oh god, you are doing my head in." The ability to ask, "What's new?" without already knowing the answer.

Oh yeah, sign me up.

First published on <u>*November 7, 2014*</u>

Beauty in the Gray

*As a newcomer to Seattle, I sometimes struggle
with the very unique weather patterns here. But I must
be getting used to it, because I actually managed
to write this sincere entry in praise of rain!*

It's another rainy Seattle day. Just as it was yesterday. And the day before. And the day before that. You don't realize how much you thrive on sunlight until it's taken from you.

I've only lived in the Pacific Northwest for a little over a year, but I'm already sensing a pattern. This time of the year, it would be quite easy to burrow beneath a heavy woolen blanket of gloom. Hibernate until Spring.

"How do you stand it, year after year?" I asked a friend.

"You have to find the beauty in the gray," he said.

And it may take some effort, but there *is* beauty in it. For one thing, because it's so gray, when you see other colors they seem unbelievably vivid. Even the red of a stop sign becomes beautiful.

You also get the feeling from all this rain that everything is cleaner, and greener, and thriving. Life, nature, is all around you. Even in this big city, you feel as though the air you are breathing is somehow better for you.

Also, the fact that it's raw and wet outside gives you an excellent excuse to snuggle up with someone. (Yeah, right. As if I need an excuse.)

And just as other colors become vivid, other seasons become vivid as well. Summer here is glorious. You find it impossible to wipe the smile off your face. You appreciate everything so much more because you know that you'll only have it for so long. You take nothing for granted.

Maybe we need to look at life, in general, this way. You only get so much of it. Savor it. If that's the lesson in the gray, then it's a true gift, indeed.

First published on <u>*November 13, 2015*</u>

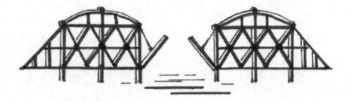

Blooming

Evolution and positive change are all the more precious and delightful when they come unexpectedly, later in life!

"I'm so glad you moved to Seattle," a friend said.

"Me too! I feel like I'm blossoming."

And it's true. In the short time I've been here, I've opened myself up, allowed myself to be vulnerable, and a lot of great things have happened in the process. I don't think I could go back to being my Florida self, even though she existed for 49 years.

You really don't expect to make yourself over from the inside out at this age, but intentional or not, it's what I've seemed to have done. Not that I'm 100 percent different. As a matter of fact, some of my traits have become even more ingrained as I've become more comfortable in my own skin. I feel as though I have a stronger sense of who I am, and am quite okay with the conclusions that I've drawn.

This is an unexpected boon at this stage of my life.

"Talk about a late bloomer!" I said to my friend.

"Nonsense! You're right on time," she replied.

What a delightful attitude. And she has a point.

Whenever you bloom, it's obviously right when you were supposed to do so.

Nature has a way of taking its course.

First published on <u>October 24, 2015</u>

Bob Cratchit is my Hero

I have to look back at this entry and smile. I no longer work on a three-bridgetender-per-shift bridge, and I now make a lot more money and am in a much more worker-friendly environment, but I'm glad I experienced that drama because it makes me grateful for its absence!

When I walked in the door today, two of my coworkers were engaged in a bit of a shouting match. It was about the room temperature. One felt it was too hot, the other felt it was just right, and what ensued was a battle royal, despite the fact that one of them would be leaving in less than 20 minutes. "Merry Christmas", I thought, as that day was less than 9 hours away.

When you work three people to a shift, trapped for 8 hours in a little room as we do on this drawbridge, a certain amount of drama is bound to ensue. For the love of all that's holy, do NOT discuss politics or religion up in here. Not if you want to escape with your life. (Well, okay, I'm exaggerating, but you get what I'm saying.) When someone turns on the news, I've learned to put on my head phones and lose myself in my music.

In honor of the season, I brought in one of the many film versions of a classic tale, *A Christmas Carol* and watched it on my laptop. It occurred to me that of all the characters in that classic story, the one who appeals to me the most is Bob Cratchit.

In many ways I can relate to him, and in many others I aspire to be him.

I relate to his circumstances. He's underpaid, and his boss (in my case, the greater corporation, because I actually like my immediate supervisor) is cheap, and is much more concerned with getting a day's work out of his employees than he is about their general welfare. My employers could so easily pay me more and change my life, and could provide decent health insurance and proper and up-to-date working equipment, but they don't care about me or anyone else. As with Scrooge, it's all about the money. We wear the chains we forge in life. No doubt about it.

But here's what impresses me about Bob Cratchit: In spite of his dismal working conditions and stress at home (a sick child, a lot of mouths to feed, and what appears to be a cranky, albeit loving spouse), he's basically very happy, and seems to have his priorities straight. Work is something you do for survival. But what you live for is friends and family. There's nothing else that matters, really–certainly not the room temperature.

In the interests of full disclosure, in spite of the lousy pay and benefits, I actually do like my job. I'd just like to be able to do more than merely survive. But maybe I should take a page from Bob Cratchit's book and stop feeling hopeless about my lot in life. Maybe I should shift my focus away from the things I want and will most likely never have, and instead realize that I already have quite a bit—a roof over my head (for now, anyway), enough food on my table, and people whom I love very much. When all is said and done, that's really all any of us need. Everything else is just stuff.

First published on <u>December 24, 2012</u>

Come On, Get Happy!

Who cares why you're happy! Just enjoy it!

I'm currently in the longest running good mood I've ever experienced in my life. Granted, the bar is set pretty low because I am prone to depression, but here lately it feels like the hills are alive with the sound of music. What can I say? I'm just happy. It feels fantastic.

I hope it's not because I've been consuming more yogurt. I read about a study that says that increasing the probiotics in your system aids with depression. Apparently bad bacteria in your gut actually sends signals to your brain which alters your mood. Probiotics replace that bad bacteria with the good kind. I figured it was worth a try. But I hope there's more to it than that. I'd hate to think I'm nothing but a vehicle that bacteria rides around in, and my outlook is dictated by who's behind that gastrointestinal steering wheel.

Or maybe it's just that it's been extremely sunny here in Seattle of late. Vitamin D is good. The days are longer, and the world is in bloom. So is a distant yellow star in control of my attitude?

I prefer another theory. For the first time in my life I took a long, hard look at myself and determined what was making me miserable, and I then made a lot of long, hard scary changes. I'm not talking about changing my hairstyle, here. I'm talking about changes that took years and cost a fortune and were extremely high risk. I basically tore my life down to its very foundations and started over again in a new place where I know not a soul. I also started seeking out life experiences. I have been reinventing myself. And dare I say it? I like how I'm turning out.

So yeah. I'm happy. Whether it's due to my own personal do-over, the sun, or to the bacterial warfare I'm waging in my stomach, or some combination of all three, I'll take it. I'll take it, and go back for seconds.

First published on May 13, 2015

Comfort Zones

As far as I'm concerned, it's important to make your comfort zone as comfortable as possible!

As much as I love to travel and explore and experience new things, I have to admit that I thrive on routine. I like to know what's coming next. I enjoy just going through the motions without having to think or plan. There's a reason it's called a comfort zone. It's quite comfortable indeed.

I'm currently in a unique position where I don't have any routine established. It doesn't help that my work schedule is so varied and insane right now that it would be hard to create one. But when I get the chance I will be making a routine from scratch. What an opportunity!

I have already decided that whenever the weather is nice I'll spend as much time as possible outdoors, because nice weather is rather rare in this neck of the woods, so I should enjoy it while I can. On those days when I get off work in the early afternoon I have been eating my dinner in the back yard while watching the dogs play. More of that, please.

And I'm trying to eat healthier, and now that I have a tub I plan to take long baths regularly. I sort of look at these things as gifts that I give to myself. I've earned that much.

I got myself a hummingbird feeder in the hopes that they would establish a routine as well, but the little guys have yet to discover it. New routines apparently take time to take hold, even in nature. But they sure do feel good when they're in place.

First published on <u>September 13, 2014</u>

Coming to the Rescue

Do we rescue our pets, or do our pets rescue us?
Either way, there's gratitude there.

I just had a long talk with my newest dog, Quagmire. Don't panic. I'm not Son of Sam. I'm willing to acknowledge that the conversation was rather one-sided. But just by being the dog that he is, he was able to tell me quite a bit.

Before I adopted him, he was found dirty, terrified, and on the street. That's no place for a little Dachshund. He had no microchip or collar, and although the rescue organization kept him for quite some time before putting him up for adoption, no one came for him. That astounds me, because in the short time I've had him in my life, I know that this dog is the pure embodiment of love. How could anyone not move heaven and earth to find him?

I will never know his whole story, but it's clear that he's been through a lot. I'm beginning to suspect there are health issues that we'll have to contend with. And he's the clingiest dog I've ever known. He has to sit in the bathroom when I take a shower, or else he'll stand outside the door and cry. He sticks to me like glue. When I come home from work, he's practically hysterical with joy. He likes to bury his little head in that space between my shoulder and my ear, deep under my hair.

I will always take good care of Quagmire. I'll keep him as healthy as I can, and I will always make sure that he feels safe and loved. My life may not be perfect, but I'm going to make his as perfect as it can possibly be.

That's one of the many joys of rescuing a pet—exercising the ability to give something the perfection that it deserves. Excellence often eludes us. As my mother loved to remind me, life isn't fair. But when you take on a pet you have the power to give them heaven on earth. You are creating your pet's entire world, and you can and should make it wonderful. That's a heady feeling, and there's no greater gift. For both of you.

First published on <u>*April 19, 2016*</u>

Concert Therapy

Every once in a while, you just have to scream in public!

I went to an Indigo Girls concert the other night and left feeling euphoric. While I love their music, I can't say I have been a classic fan. I don't buy their albums or follow them closely, so I couldn't sing along with any but their most popular songs. I'm sort of a lazy enthusiast, if that makes any sense at all. I've seen them in concert once before and had a fantastic time, so I knew I'd enjoy myself this time, too.

But I left thinking, "What is it about concerts in general?" I always leave a concert feeling sated, relaxed, and happy. I'd love to have that state of mind all the time. And here's what I think it is: only in a concert are you allowed to scream and sing at the top of your lungs, and generally make a fool of yourself in public, and that's SUCH a release. And then there's the fact that every person around you is doing the same thing, and there's also this general agreement about your current experience, and that is something we as a society seem to feel less and less with each passing day.

Everyone who is at a concert is there because they want to be. We're all on the same page. We're in this together. It's almost like a weight is lifted from everyone's shoulders. Freedom!

If concerts could be made in pill form, there would be peace on earth.

First published on <u>March 30, 2013</u>

Discarded Futures

When I wrote this blog entry, I was on the brink of monumental change. I had just moved into a new house a month prior to that, but then got an incredible job offer on the other side of the country, where I knew no one. There's nothing like that amazing feeling of being on the brink of an awesome adventure!

It's ironic that I'm about to move again, because I just moved into *this* place a month ago. But this job offer is too good to pass up. I'm excited. I'm dreading loading up my stuff again. And I have GOT to get rid of things. I can no longer lug long playing records from pillar to post when I don't even own a record player anymore. Why do I need reference books when I can get all the info I need on line? I've got so much to do.

But when I stop to catch my breath, I look around at this house and think about how much I like it. Even though I've only been here a month, I feel like I could really have made a nice home here. I feel safe here. I like that I can hear the neighbor's roosters crowing, even though I'm in the middle of the largest city by land mass on the planet. I like playing in the yard with the dogs. I can see a future here, but I've chosen to forego it.

I sometimes think about the various futures I've chosen not to pursue. It's not really a feeling of regret that comes over me, even though some of those futures might have been wonderful. It's more like a feeling of awe. There are so many possibilities out there. So many paths I can take, or could have taken.

Every life on this planet is unique. Imagine that. We are each the architects of our own evolution. Every single choice you make opens up a whole new world to you. What a gift. What a precious, precious gift.

First published on <u>August 2, 2014</u>

Donating Yourself

If you live a life of gratitude, the next step is to pay it forward! And there are many ways to do that without depleting your bank account.

Times are tough and there's so much need out there that it can be overwhelming. But it's understandable when people can't make financial donations. I for one am struggling to make ends meet. But there are so many other ways to help.

Here are some ways you can give of yourself, show the world how wonderful you are, and improve the lives of others without spending a dime, and if you need added incentive, in many cases you can write these donations off on your taxes.

Become a marrow donor. If you're between the ages of 18 and 44, a simple cheek swab will get you registered, and if you become a match it could save someone's life. Go here to order a registration kit.

Become a cord blood donor. Are you pregnant? Donating your baby's cord blood after birth does not put you or your child at risk and could save someone's life. Talk to your doctor and find out if your hospital participates in this program before your child is born. For more information, go here.

Donate your used clothing and furniture. It breaks my heart to see useable items on the curb on trash day when there are so many organizations that would be happy to take them off your hands. Many will even come and pick them up from you.

Donate your used car. There are a lot of organizations that will take your used car. donateacar.com can connect you to various charitable organizations, but personally, I plan to donate my car to npr.org when the time comes.

Volunteer. Many organizations in your community could use your help. volunteermatch.org can help you find those opportunities.

Give someone a micro-loan. I can't say enough about Kiva.org. In a nutshell, loan 25 dollars, change someone's life, get paid back, and hopefully do it again. What have you got to lose? Not one single penny, that's what.

Help a neighbor. If you have a neighbor who is sick or elderly or disabled or a single parent, they could no doubt use your help. Whether it's shoveling snow, running an errand, doing home repair or mowing the lawn, there are any number of things you could do to make their lives easier.

Donate blood. Another free opportunity to save a life! Imagine that. Go to redcrossblood.org to find the blood bank nearest you.

Freecycle. One man's trash is another man's treasure. Rather than filling the landfill with your perfectly usable but no longer wanted items, advertise them here on your local freecycle.org network This is a great way to pick up things that other people are giving away as well!

Spread the word. Do you know of a way for people to save money or live healthier or safer lives? Don't keep this information to yourself. Share it. Facebook it. Tweet it. Whatever it takes to share this with others. Knowledge is power.

Donate your hair. Planning to cut more than 10 inches of your hair off? Don't let it go to waste! There are organizations that will make wigs for people who have cancer or alopecia. I don't want to give any one organization special treatment, so simply google "hair donation" and choose the one you like best.

Listen. Sometimes all someone needs to turn their day around is someone willing to listen to them. Really hear them. That's a skill. Please practice it.

Participate in Neighborhood Watch. Help keep your neighborhood safe the RIGHT way, with an organization that does not advocate vigilante behavior. Google Neighborhood Watch to learn more.

Be a mentor. Share your knowledge and expertise with someone who would benefit from it. Learn more about this at mentoring.org.

Recycle. Think of this as volunteering for the planet.

Report abuse and other crimes when you see them. If you witness domestic violence or any other crime, speak up. That's the only way you'll prevent its recurrence. This is a way of doing a good turn for a future victim. Simply dial 911, or if you are outside of the United States, find out your emergency number and keep it handy.

Be an organ donor. Sign up to become an organ donor in your state's organ donor registry and you will not have died in vain. (www.organdonor.gov/becomingdonor/)Also, be sure to share your wishes with your loved ones so that there's no conflict or confusion when the time comes.

There are so many ways to make a difference in this world, and you don't have to spend any money doing so.

I do 13 of the things mentioned above, but doing even one will make the world a better place. Join me, won't you?

Remember when you were young and willing? It's never too late.

First published on January 23, 2014

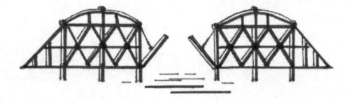

Don't Underestimate the Elderly

Looking back at this blog entry fills me with irony, because that "delightful" landlady turned out to be a total nightmare, but I'm still grateful for the inspiration she provided to me at the time. Even false perceptions can provide wonderful lessons!

My landlady is 72 years old, and only 4 months out from heart surgery, and yet the first time I saw her, she was wearing short shorts, a tank top, and a half ton of jewelry.

I'm convinced she's in better shape than I am. I think she's delightful.

Back in the 80's, I used to work in this mom and pop video rental store. (This was before Blockbuster came along and wiped them off the map.) Every week this little old lady would come in and rent 10 porn videos. I used to think, "You give me hope for the future."

I recently graduated from college with an 80-year old man who was getting his 10th degree.

The pastor of my church, in his late 60's, rode his bicycle across America this summer to raise money for charity.

My next door neighbor, may she rest in peace, lived alone until she was 95, and loved it. She rode her bike 30 miles a day until she was 80. She only stopped because she was afraid she'd fall and break a hip. So after that, she walked her dogs several miles a day.

I was talking to an 83-year-old woman about her new boyfriend. She said, "But no sex, honey. He has prostate issues." I just love her!

I know a man in his 80's who makes stained glass, takes math classes just for the heck of it, is the world's greatest cook and can touch his toes before I even start to bend over.

I work full-time with 5 people in their 70's.

Before I moved recently, I attended a yoga class with 50 people. The average age in there must have been 75, and they could all "downward dog" me under the table. It was kind of embarrassing, to tell the truth.

After being faced with so many examples of amazing elderly people, I have to ask myself, "Why do I continue to be amazed?" Why can't I get that stereotypical image of the "I've fallen and I can't get up" woman out of my head? Clearly that stereotype does them a disservice.

Yes, there are plenty of elderly people out there with health problems or dementia or an inability to care for themselves. But can you imagine how frustrating it must be for the ones I've described above to be discounted, ignored, or otherwise treated like a three year old child? I resolve, from this day forward, to approach every elderly person as if they were amazing, because more often than not, they are. Who's with me?

First published on <u>December 9, 2012</u>

Dumb Luck

It's always a good idea to count your blessings,
even if you don't win the lottery.

I've never considered myself to be a particularly lucky person.
I've never hit more than two numbers on the lottery. I've never
bought a dusty item at a yard sale that turned out to be worth
millions (or even hundreds). I've never dated anyone who
didn't turn out to be just as bat sh** crazy as I am. I've never
gotten in on the ground floor of a really lucrative investment.
I've never inherited anything of note. I'm not outstandingly
beautiful, and Lord knows I don't have the metabolism of a
hummingbird. I've never caught a baseball while sitting in the
stands.

But the other day I had a sneezing fit while going down the
highway in rush hour traffic, and when it was over I realized I'd
probably gone the length of two football fields with my eyes
closed, surrounded on all sides by other cars. It's good to be
alive.

And I always seem to manage to get the best dogs on the
planet. What are the odds?

I am employed at a time when jobs are hard to come by.

I have been born white and American at a time when that
seems to accord me privileges that I didn't earn and mostly do
not deserve.

So far, knock on wood, I haven't had any life-threatening health issues. I've even managed to make it through major surgery. And now I have decent health insurance.

I have the best sister in the world, and the most amazing friends.

And best of all, because of this blog and the many wonderful readers all over the planet (including you) and because of my StoryCorps interview and the many amazing and talented people who have entered my life since then, this anthology now exists.

So I guess I'm pretty darned lucky after all!

First published on <u>*February 1, 2014*</u>

Fame

You may not realize it, but you're someone's hero.

My friend Carole quoted a show called the Vampire Mob the other day. "We are all famous to a few people." Now, I've never been a big follower of this whole vampire phenomenon, but it appears that pearls of wisdom can be found just about anywhere.

This had me thinking about the concept of fame. To a small child, a mother is the most famous person in the world. She is, after all, his first relationship, and the purveyor of food and safety and love. She who gave you life is deserving of a certain level of fame.

But you can also be famous, for a brief shining moment, to the little old lady whom you help cross the street, or the homeless person to whom you give a blanket, or the driver of the car that you let cross in front of you during rush hour. These people will probably forget you in no time, but at that particular moment, you are their hero. Such a wonderful return for what should be very little effort. What a rush!

Most fame is short lived. Do you remember who won the show *Big Brother* in 2003? I didn't until I Googled it just now. I couldn't have picked 'em out of a line up. But at the time I had spent the summer watching this person, getting to know what they decided to reveal, at least the parts that did not wind up on the cutting room floor. But now I can't even recall if I was happy or irritated that she won. I'm sure she's a nice person. She's just not a part of my emotional solar system anymore.

Fame is also a matter of context. If you had plopped Fred Astaire down amongst the Bushmen of the Kalahari, they'd have been much more fascinated that there was a pasty-faced white man in their midst than they would have been at his ability to cut a rug. I think I would find that to be a huge relief if I had found myself in his dancing shoes. I don't thrive under scrutiny.

There's also the kind of fame that you wish you didn't have, when you do or say something incredibly stupid and draw the wrath of your corner of society. Not everyone wants to be famous, and it depends greatly on the brand and duration of that fame. Most of us, however, would like to be remembered.

Today, take a moment to reflect upon your impact on the world, and embrace your fame.

First published on June 3, 2014

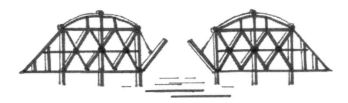

Free Hugs

*Amazing how a simple t-shirt can provide you
with some profound life lessons.*

I saw a Free Hugs t-shirt for sale on line at a fairly reasonable
price, and I said to myself, "I gotta get me one of those!" (Yes, I
know. My grammar sometimes flies out the window when I'm
speaking to myself. So sue me. I usually know what I mean.)

Since then I've worn it a couple of times, most notably at the
recent Seattle Pridefest on Capitol Hill. I figured that after the
Orlando shootings, people were going to need hugs. I knew I
did.

I must have been hugged by 20 strangers that day. What an
amazing experience. Some would come up and shyly ask for a
hug. Others would see me from a distance, throw their arms
wide, and rush at me like a linebacker. Those made me laugh as
well as smile. During each hug, we'd say, "Happy Pride!!!"

I feel healthier, happier, for having spread some love. I think
this has become my shirt of choice for all large gatherings. It
was kind of funny because my nephew was visiting from out of
town, and half the time when someone would hug me, he'd
assume it was someone I knew, and he'd be mildly insulted
that I didn't introduce him. Then he'd remember the shirt.

One time I even forgot about the shirt myself, and this guy in a
slightly rougher part of town came at me with arms
outstretched, and I briefly thought the worst. I think that may

have hurt his feelings, and I still feel bad about it. That hug did not feel as good as it should have. I wish I could turn back time and give him a more genuine hug. That shirt brings with it a certain responsibility that I hadn't anticipated.

That caused me to wonder what would happen if someone wanted to hug me whom I didn't want to hug, someone very dirty or with open sores and rotting teeth or something. What would I do? My shirt didn't say, "Free hugs unless you look like you could be contagious."

I have to admit that some of the huggers, after a day-long festival in the bright sunshine, didn't smell as good as they probably usually did, but I still found the experience worth it. And in the end, the hug gods seemed to be watching over me. Everyone who came up to me seemed to do it with an open heart and a genuine spirit.

I did see several people look at my shirt and then hesitate a bit. I think they wanted a hug but were afraid to go for it. I'd smile at them, but I certainly didn't want to cause discomfort. A hug should never be forced. I hope I at least planted the seed in them for the next free hugger who crosses their path.

Sending you a virtual hug, dear reader, if you want one. We're all in this together, after all.

First published on July 5, 2016

Gaining Your Temper

Your perspective can temper your attitude. What a gift.

Temper
[tem-per] noun
1. habit of mind, especially with respect to irritability or patience, outbursts of anger, or the like; disposition: an even temper.
2. heat of mind or passion, shown in outbursts of anger, resentment, etc.
3. a substance added to something to modify its properties or qualities.

Everyone loses their temper once in a while. Lately I've had quite a lot to be angry about. I've experienced injustices of a personal, societal and political nature, and I've also made some epic mistakes. Sometimes it's hard not to be perpetually pissed off.

Your temper is something you're taught you should never lose, but that leads me to believe that it's something you must first have. You can't lose something you don't possess, and apparently it's valuable or the whole world wouldn't be urging you to hang on to it. So I started thinking about this thing, this temper, and what it means to have it and to lose it.

If you look at definition number three above, you'll note that a temper modifies you. Think of tempered steel. It's stronger and harder than regular steel. It's also magnetic. I want those qualities. I want a backbone of tempered steel. I want to be able to withstand the slings and arrows of life. I want to persevere. I want to endure.

The temper is also contradictory. You can be even tempered, or you can have a temper, which means you're prone to fits of anger. I like the idea that a temper can be what you make it, that you have choices.

I am going to try to let my temper temper me. I am going to attempt to let my righteous indignation about injustices make me stronger. I'm going to make an effort to stand up straight and make choices about the woman I want to be.

I want to gain my temper.

First published on December 4, 2013

Generational Changes

What a difference a generation can make, and how lucky
we are to stand on the shoulders of our ancestors!

Recently I had the good fortune to meet a distant cousin. Her maternal great-grandfather and my paternal great-grandfather were brothers. And all this time she's lived about 5 miles from me. Talk about a small world.

That part of the family comes from France, and as we talked over lunch, a few things struck me. In the space of one generation, not only did my branch of the family tree completely change languages, but we also altered the way our family name is pronounced.

The language thing makes sense. Of course you're going to adopt the language of the country in which you live. And even if you don't or can't, your children surely will. It's inevitable.

But the name pronunciation change intrigues me. Why did that happen? Did some relative simply get tired of correcting people? Or perhaps it was an effort to try to seem less foreign, or try to fit in.

How long did it take before the new pronunciation started to feel normal? I wonder.

Another thing that really hit home for me as I bid my newfound cousin adieu was the very miracle that any of us become who we are. Think about it. If some distant relative decided to say home instead of going to that dance where he met his future wife, a whole branch of the human family would not exist. If grandma had turned left instead of right on a fateful day, she would have never met grandpa. If some ancient ancestor had been attacked by a saber-toothed tiger, poof! Your whole family history would be history.

We are all a product of centuries of pure coincidence. Yes, each generation slightly alters the path on which your family treads, but hundreds of people had to survive and meet to make you who you are today. What a gift!

First published on <u>May 22, 2016</u>

Generosity Breeds Abundance

*I suppose this is a fancy way of saying
what goes around comes around,
but that doesn't make it any less genuine!*

It seems rather simple to me. The more you give, the more likely you will be to receive. And even when I don't receive, I just feel better when I give.

One of the things I try to do regularly is send out kudos e-mails at work. I don't know why people find it so hard to recognize and compliment the good works of others, but since I know I appreciate it when people do that for me, I try to do it for others as well. I'll write the e-mail to their supervisor, my supervisor, the division head, and the person in question. I'll simply state the good work that was done and how much it is appreciated. I'll only do this if I sincerely feel it. (People can tell when you're being fake.)

I also try to keep in mind what people find interesting, and then when I hear something new about that topic, I share it with them. People genuinely like being thought about. I know I do. When someone says, "This made me think of you," it feels like a hug to me.

I've known plenty of selfish people in my lifetime. What I've observed is that when you turf guard or hoard the good things for yourself, or put your needs ahead those of everyone else, people stop trusting you. They don't like you. They'll hesitate to help you in your time of need. And you will therefore become even more bitter, selfish and angry. It's a downward spiral.

The best way to stay off that spiral is to give, even if you're fairly certain you'll get nothing in return. Give, even when it doesn't feel pleasant. Give, and let the universe take care of whether that giving was deserved. It's not always easy. But in the end you, and everyone in your circle of influence, will be much better for it.

First published on February 24, 2016

Generosity

*It's not always easy to be generous, but making
the effort shows what you're made of.*

I can always tell when my coworkers are burned out. They stop
coming to work early. In fact, some of them will arrive a few
minutes early but wait in their cars, only coming in at the last
possible moment.

They are perfectly within their rights to do so, of course, but
what that means is the person on the shift they are relieving
can't leave until they arrive. I know personally that when I've
had a long day, being able to leave even five minutes early is a
gift. Because I know this, I try very hard to show up early for
others. It's an easy gift to give.

But I can understand the thought process. "Why should I work
5 minutes for free?" "So and so never comes in early for me.
Why should I come in early for him?" "I am tired of giving and
getting nothing back." It's particularly hard to be generous
when the recipient is someone you don't like.

But that's when generosity stops being generosity. When it
becomes all about "What's in it for me?" and not a sincere act of
kindness without a scorecard, it gets sick and twisted and
unhealthy.

If sometimes you get fed up because it seems like you're being
taken advantage of on all sides, consider this: These are the
moments when you get to show what you're truly made of. If

your first instinct is to withdraw kindness, then you've just done some damage, yes, but not to those around you.

I try to be generous without giving it much thought. Sometimes I struggle with this. Sometimes I have to force myself to be generous in spite of my baser instincts. I know in these situations I'm just going through the motions and being insincere. But I think it's important to keep up this emotional muscle memory, because I never want to become one of those people who waits in her car until the last possible minute.

First published on <u>April 5, 2015</u>

Generosity Makes an Impact

*There's no greater way to show your gratitude
than by paying it forward.*

Recently I pulled up to the gate at a tourist attraction, stupidly surprised that I'd have to pay for parking, and realizing that this meant I'd probably have to go without lunch because in my world, every penny counts and there aren't that many pennies available.

And then the parking attendant said, "Go on through. The guy ahead of you paid for both of you." Now, understand that this was a complete stranger to me, and he had no idea how big an impact he was making. I tried to keep track of his vehicle during our individual hunts for a parking space so that I could thank him, but we got separated. But I'll never forget that gesture.

I know, because it's not the first time I've been the recipient of such generosity. One time I was visiting my mother in Las Vegas and discovered that at the time, about 23 years ago, you could pay 100 dollars to fly from there through the Grand Canyon, then take a shuttle to the rim, and stay in a hotel and fly back the next day. That was a lot of money at the time, but I'd never been to the Grand Canyon. How could I resist? So off I went on this amazing adventure.

Taking the shuttle from the rim I learned that the hotel was at a bit of a remove, and I was chatting with the shuttle driver to see what there was to do near the hotel that evening. We passed an Imax theater, and I said something along the lines of, "I could go to that, but how much does it cost?" He said it was 8 dollars. I probably sighed, because I only had 5 dollars. Oh well. As he pulled up to the hotel and I was getting off, he handed me a 10 dollar bill and said, "Enjoy the Imax." I was so touched. When I got home I wrote a letter to his boss so he'd know what an amazing employee he had. And whenever I think of the Grand Canyon, I think of that man, who just wanted to make a total stranger smile.

If I ever am in the financial place to do so, I intend to pay these things forward. It doesn't take that much, really, to reaffirm someone's faith in humanity. Try it.

First published on September 24, 2013

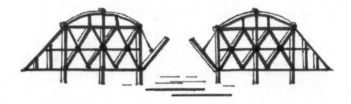

Give Yourself a Raise

I am grateful to finally have a union job, but if you aren't as fortunate, all is not lost.

Recently I got a raise at work, and I was thrilled. You have to understand. For 14 years I worked in a non-union job, and we got a one dollar raise every 6 years, which, needless to say, did not keep pace with the cost of living. And we'd have to fight to get that. We also got 3000 dollars' worth of health coverage a year, which barely covered prescriptions for most of us. Now I'm working the same job on the other side of the country and we have a union and I'm earning three times as much, with a benefit package that moves me to tears whenever I contemplate it.

Let's face it, if employers actually cared about their workers, there'd be no need for unions. Assuming The Man is going to behave honorably without union oversight is pure fantasy. Without unions there would still be sweat shops, child labor, and 80 hour work weeks.

I realize I'm one of the lucky ones. I just kind of fell into this good fortune. I did nothing special to deserve it. I was just in the right place at the right time. I am no more worthy than you are. I wish I could share this luck with every single person on the planet, but that's not within my power.

But please don't overlook or discount the power that you do have. There's much about our quality of life that only we can control. We may be stuck in a system that is rigged against us, but there are plenty of ways that we can raise ourselves up.

Find something that you love doing outside of work and do it just for the pure joy of it. You might also consider thinking of ways to make money by doing it, but that's definitely not required.

Volunteer. This will give you a great deal of satisfaction. Call it a karma raise. And though your efforts you may meet people and make contacts that will translate into a future job, or make like-minded friends. You can never have too many of those.

Be ever mindful that the best things in life don't cost a penny. Love. Friendship. Learning. Beauty. Reach out for those things. Embrace them.

Vote! Make your opinion count! Be heard!

Whenever possible, do as much as you can to lift up the people around you. Acknowledge their efforts. Give compliments. Be generous. That abundance will come back to you. On the other hand, turf-guarding, selfishness and subjugation will drag you down as well.

No one can treat you as well as you can treat yourself. But are you doing that? Being kind to yourself, pampering yourself? Our culture may frown upon it, but it's the greatest gift you can give yourself. Make it a habit.

Speak your truth. Embrace your uniqueness. Maintain your integrity. Do what feels right to you. All these things will make you a more authentic, happy individual, and when you live that happiness, good things will come your way. No one can take that away from you.

Explore your spirituality to its natural (for you) conclusion. Therein lies peace.

Exercise. Do yoga. Walk in the world. Actively play.

Do something to give yourself a raise every day. It's every bit as important to you as food. Think of it as feeding your spirit. The Man isn't in charge of your well-being. You are.

First published on <u>April 18, 2016</u>

Barb Abelhauser

Have a Little Faith

You can't control your external validations,
but you can provide validation for others.

There are certain things that I long to hear from people that I care about.

I have faith in you.
I'm proud of you.
I trust you.
You can do it.
I appreciate you.
I love you.

Yes, it's always dangerous to rely on outside sources for your personal validation, but as far as I can tell, most people crave it. That's why Facebook is so popular. There's something addictive to having people "like" your opinions. We naturally prefer to be agreed with.

Sadly, many people seem to withhold the above statements even when they feel it. And if you have to ask, "Do you trust me?" you come away feeling slightly pathetic. So you don't ask, and you don't know.

Unfortunately, you cannot control external validation. But if you want it, you can be sure that others do, too. And you *can* control that. Tell the people that you love that you are proud of them, trust them, have faith in them. Let them know. If you do, then maybe, just maybe, they'll pay it forward to someone else.

You could have an impact beyond your own intimate circle of friends and relatives.

Having said that, I appreciate you, dear reader. Namaste.

First published on <u>May 9, 2015</u>

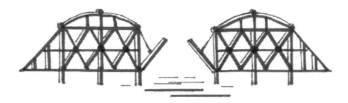

Congratulations, You're Alive!

Even if I do say so myself, this blog entry always gives me butterflies of excitement. It's a reminder to celebrate the uniqueness of you!

Do you ever think about the miracle of your existence? It's incredible, really. The odds of you... *you* actually being here to read this blog are greater than being struck by lightning.

Think of the one hundred generations that had to to procreate before you were even born. They had to survive plagues and wars and pestilence and catastrophe and childbirth. They had to be smart enough not to fatally injure themselves, and mentally healthy enough not to end it all. They had to meet just the right person to produce just the right child that would then meet just the right person... and so on. If even just one of those guys had spent just 5 extra minutes in the bushes or the outhouse or the bathroom on the day he was destined to meet his life partner, he may have met someone else and this current version of you wouldn't exist.

And even before that, the planet had to develop in just the right way to sustain life. The primordial ooze had to be just oozy enough. The earth had to be the correct distance from the sun. It had to have water and develop plants and animals. Our ancestors had to be great swimmers, then great crawlers, then great climbers, then great runners. The dinosaurs had to be wiped out. The continents had to divide. The climate had to be just right in order for us to survive.

No wonder we have such high opinions of ourselves! What a miracle it is to be alive! What a precious gift!

Let's try really hard not to screw it up for the generations to come, shall we?

First published on <u>*May 16, 2014*</u>

Have an Awful Day

Live for the moment! Revel in it! Appreciate the now!

It's fascinating how the definition of some words evolves over time to signify the opposite of their original meaning. Awful originally meant "full of awe." I miss that definition. If we allowed awful to fulfill its original role, people would stop saying awesome. I, for one, would be thrilled, because awesome is a word which annoys me for purely aesthetic reasons, although I admit I have resorted to using it more than once myself.

But as usual, I digress. I would like you, dear reader, to have a day full of awe. Take a moment every once in a while today to come to a complete halt. If you need a reminder to do this thing that is so foreign to your routine, set the alarm on your cell phone if you must, but take the opportunity to let this fast-paced world in which we live swirl around you and past you while you stand still and look around. Become the still point in the turning world. You will be amazed at what you see.

I'm talking about stopping to smell the roses writ large. Appreciate the flowers at your feet, yes, but also the sun on your face and the wind in your hair and the clothes upon your back and the food on your plate. Be grateful for your health if you have it, and your friends and your coworkers and the fact that you get to be here, right here, right now, breathing and living. That's a very significant accomplishment, and it takes a lot of intricate things falling into place just right in order for it to be possible.

Appreciate the complexity of life. Appreciate the simplicity of life. Realize that graffiti can often be beautiful and even the most irritating situation has something to teach you. Use all five of your senses if you can, and enjoy the fact that you have them.

It would be easy to take the next step and start talking about spirituality and higher powers and all the religious trappings that go with those. But for this moment, this "right here", just this once, don't focus on that. Just concentrate on feeling the awe of this amazing gift you've been given, without trying to read the return address on the package.

Here's wishing you a truly, wondrously, spectacularly awful day!

First published on <u>May 30, 2014</u>

Having What I Need

Focusing on what you don't have is the killer of contentment.

I had another epiphany last night. (I know. Watch out!)

I can't afford to adequately heat my home, but I have a warm sleeping bag, a comfortable bed, a roof to keep the rain off my head, and walls to (more or less) block out the wind.

I'm starved for human contact, but my dog spoons with me every night and is an excellent source of unconditional love.

I'm not rich, but I'm not worried about where my next meal is coming from as I sometimes have been in the past.

The epiphany was this: I have everything I need. If I focus on that instead of on all the things that I want but don't have, I'll be a lot more content.

Millions of people in this world don't have what they need. It's a precious gift that I do. Yes, I've worked hard to get where I am, but I have to admit that when all is said and done, I am blessed with good fortune.

Everything is okay.

First published on February 26, 2016

Here I Am

I am not a hard person to give a gift to. It won't even cost you a dime. The best gifts in life are free.

When I was a little kid, my self-esteem was so low that I actually thought that when I was out of people's sight, I no longer existed for them. Kind of like my own personal Schrödinger's cat thought experiment, I had to be observed to be sure I was actually alive.

Needless to say with age I have become more grounded in reality and more confident, but to this day when someone does something nice for me outside of my presence, it never fails to bring happy tears to my eyes, sentimental fool that I am. It could be something as simple as picking me up something that I like at the grocery store even though I haven't asked for it, or saying, "I saw this help wanted ad and thought you might be perfect for it." Anything that implies that someone was thinking of me when I wasn't there…that's very precious to me.

I guess the moral of this story is that everybody wants to be appreciated and remembered and acknowledged, so I try to do that for others as often as I can.

First published on May 27, 2013

Hold on to your Highest Point

*Even when you are at your lowest point,
you still have your memories.*

I'm having a really, really bad few days. They come, they go.
The older you get, the more you realize it's not the end of the
world. The pendulum always swings back the other direction
eventually.

So, on days like this, when my boss shows his true a**hole
colors, the man in my life has no concept of the term emotional
support, the dogs are misbehaving, I'm sliding closer and closer
to the abyss of homelessness and my landlord doesn't seem to
want me to live where I live anymore, I think of my highest
point, and hold on to it as tightly as I can. That's what I
recommend for everyone.

I'm particularly lucky in that I happen to have one of my
highest points on film. It's a photo of me in San Marco Square
in Venice, Italy, 2006. I have a pigeon on my head and another
on my chest and I look like I've never been happier in my life.

It took me years of sacrifice and determination to get there,
and yet there I stand, about to be pooped on by pigeons,
despite all financial odds. I made that happen. No one helped.
And no one can take that from me. That photo will always
remind me of that fact.

When you are standing in a dark valley of despair, it's nice to
be able to look up at a high pinnacle, illuminated by sunlight,

and remember that at some point in time, you were standing there instead.

First published on <u>March 6, 2013</u>

Home is Where?

I wrote this when I had only been in Seattle for 3 months, and still didn't know a soul. Since then it has become my home and I love it here. I'm grateful that this place has embraced me.

I'm starting to settle in to Seattle. I'm beginning to sort of know my way around. I've figured out where a lot of the different neighborhoods are located. I know which grocery stores I prefer. I know when to avoid the interstate (which is pretty much all of the time). I have gotten my library card and my driver license. I've voted.

It still feels a little like a foreign country to me, though. Given the fact that I love to travel more than anything in the world, that's a high compliment. But I often dress inappropriately for this weather. I don't know how things work. I often feel like people are speaking a foreign language and I don't quite get how things are supposed to be done. There comes a time in every trip when you long for home. I have those days.

But the fact is I have been feeling rather transient for the past 4 or 5 years. That's not Seattle's fault. I think selling my house was the defining moment. That's when I pulled up anchor and started drifting. I like having a home I can call my own that I can alter or remodel or neglect as I see fit, without the worry of being evicted by anyone other than the bank.

I also like having a sense of community. I like having a group of friends and a church that I feel a part of, and a strong understanding of the local gossip, politics, insider jokes and slang. I enjoy having certain traditions that I hold every year, such as attending annual festivals. I definitely do not have any of that here yet.

I think home for me is ownership, knowledge, routine, tradition, and community. It's fitting in. It's feeling comfortable and anchored. I'm sure I'll get there eventually.

There's no place like home.

First published on November 20, 2014

How Delicious It Is to Feed Your Ego

Revel in your special gifts.

There's nothing more satisfying than doing something you're really good at. That feeling when everything falls into place. That sense of being in the zone. It's almost like you have a calling. For a brief shining moment, you are superhuman.

Whether we know it or not, we all have a talent. If you think you don't, you simply haven't identified yours yet. It might be something basic, such as making the best pancakes. Or it could be something more complex, like having the ability to memorize pi to the 22,000th digit. But you have a certain something, I guarantee you. Ask friends and family, "What am I good at?" You'll see a pattern emerge.

I used to know a guy who made the most amazing pottery you've ever seen. I haven't spoken to him for about 20 years, but I still have some of his pots sitting on my shelf. His was a rare talent, and it made me crazy that he had absolutely no plan to make something of it. He used to say to me, "Just because you're good at something doesn't mean you have to do it." And in fact, he became an electrician. You'd think he'd at least have a pottery wheel in his garage, but no.

I don't think you have to make a living from your special abilities, whatever they may be, but it's a great disservice to your soul and to the wider world if you don't exercise the gifts you are given in some capacity. Let your light shine.

First published on <u>March 23, 2014</u>

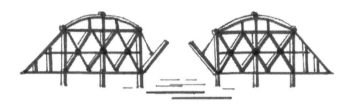

How This Blog Has Touched Me

I knew that writing a blog would have an impact on me, but I didn't realize what a big part my readers would play in my life. I am so grateful for every single one of you.

Today this blog made me cry. It wasn't the first time. I'm sure it won't be the last.

So far it's always been happy tears, thank goodness. (I'm waiting for the day that my writer's block is so overwhelming that I shed tears of sheer frustration, but so far I've been lucky.) Still, I never thought this humble project of mine would bring out such strong emotion in me. Had I known, I might have been too intimidated to start. But I'm so glad I did.

This time, the reason for my tears was a comment from a girl named April. She read one of my more popular blog entries, <u>Why I Hate Alcohol</u>. Then she commented in great detail about how it impacted her.

Discovering that something I wrote has helped someone, or made them look at things from a different angle, or taught someone something they didn't know, never fails to move me. Sometimes I sit up here on my lonely little drawbridge and then I write about the things I have seen; and it almost feels as if I'm putting messages in bottles and throwing them in the ocean. That these messages sometimes reach someone's shore is gratifying beyond words.

Because of this blog, I've also made some amazing friends. Art, Carole, Anju, Sonia, Tony, Lyn, Valarie... so many more I couldn't list them all, but each one an amazing person that wouldn't have come into my life without this forum. And then there are the many friends I've met in other ways who have followed this blog and given me feedback and support. There's nothing more wonderful than getting positive encouragement from someone you admire.

I've also learned a great deal. I've explored topics I wouldn't have bothered to delve into if I didn't think I'd have some reader to share them with. I've introduced myself, and you, to people I would not have discovered otherwise.

I've exorcised a number of personal demons, celebrated a number of victories, shared perhaps more than I should have, and wondered about any number of things. And I've improved my writing skills. Those are things I knew I would do. What I didn't know was that having people actually read what I write has added a whole new dimension. You've validated, supported, and commiserated with me. You've given me wings.

And when I look at my readership and realize that it extends around the globe, I am in awe. These messages in bottles that I send out each day have traveled far and wide, and that means so much to me. Whether you're in Egypt or Singapore or Mexico or here in the United States, the very fact that you have taken time out of your day to read my words is a precious gift that I am honored to receive.

So my message in the bottle for today is: Thank you. Thank you so much.

First published on January 6, 2016

Human Contact

There's no better way to connect with people, and with the wider world, than by doing so face to face.

The other night I had sort of a girls' night out with a new friend. We had dinner, and then went to a storytelling/music event. I had a wonderful time. It was nice to talk to someone face to face who wasn't a coworker. It's been a long time. I've been entirely too isolated.

It was a beautiful evening, and we ate at a sidewalk café, and then went to a broiling hot venue to hear really good stories and really horrible music. The heat was so oppressive that I nearly passed out, but you know what? It was worth it.

There's a lot to be said for human contact. It's nice to have a touch stone, someone with whom to share your opinions, get feedback, and hear new perspectives. It's also great to get out of your head for a while, and hear someone else's stories and experiences. You can learn a lot that way.

It's very easy, in this cyber world, to go for long stretches of time talking to people only via e-mail or Facebook or whatever. It's contact, yes, but it's an illusion. It can't replace looking someone in the eye, or hearing someone's voice, or sharing a plate of fried broccoli as you watch people walk by.

It's easy to take the internet shortcut. We are all so busy and the world is so fast-paced. It takes a lot less effort to reach out in a virtual way. I'm not saying that you should stop your on-line activities, but if you take the time to have real contact, you reap many rewards. So maybe it's time to turn off your computer and pick up the phone and invite someone for coffee. Just a thought.

First published on June 12, 2015

Human Signposts

I'm always fascinated by the way the people who cross your path can alter your course, in both good ways and bad. Either way, it's all a part of this wonderful journey.

As you walk your path in life, you'll come across many intersections and forks in the road, and you'll have to make decisions. Sometimes you won't even know you're at a crossroad until you look back and realize you've negotiated your way through it, or discover to your horror that you've gotten off track and have to go back and start again.

At times like this it's really good to be a human being, because you have the power to observe and communicate and learn from others. Look around you and you'll realize that there are human signposts at nearly every turn. Some people are admirable and you want to emulate them. Follow their path as much as you possibly can. Others are bad influences. They should have "Do Not Enter" tattooed across their foreheads. Many people are excellent sources of advice, and you can often learn from their past mistakes if you only take the time to listen to them.

When I come across a toxic individual, I try to comfort myself with the fact that I'm learning a valuable lesson about how I do *not* want to be. It's as if they've done the screwing up for me, and yet I can still add it to my life experience. Toxic people can cause you a lot of heartache, but they can save you from even more of it as you walk away from them a much wiser individual.

Take the time to really observe the people who touch your life. Every single one is a sign post. Every single one has value.

First published on <u>*February 11, 2015*</u>

I Am Not Who I was Yesterday

Every day is a do-over! What a gift!

It's been an eventful week. I won't bore you with the details. Suffice it to say that it has served to remind me that we are all the sum total of our unique life experiences. That being the case, since we experience life every single day, that means that we are each slightly different than we were the day before. The onion has another layer. What a concept.

I find this idea rather comforting. To me, it means that with each new day comes another opportunity to get things right. It allows me to look at the world with fresh eyes, and make new choices. If there's something about myself that I want to change, I can tackle that thing from a slightly different trajectory. If there's something I want to strengthen or reinforce, here's another chance to do so.

Each day we burst forth from our chrysalis and spread our wings as a brand new butterfly. As my late boyfriend used to say, "You have been given a perfectly good day. What are you going to do with it?" That saying is even more poignant now that he is gone.

Never take your fresh starts for granted, people. Each and every one is precious.

First published on June 8, 2016

I Just Love a Good Glottal Stop

Ah, the pure aural delight of the human voice!

I was just listening to a friend who hails from Essex, England. What was he talking about? I have no idea. Oh, I could understand him. It's just that I was so mesmerized by the sound of his voice that I really wasn't focusing on the content of his commentary. He could read the phone book and I would sit happily entranced at his feet. You see, I love a good glottal stop.

A glottal stop is that sort of hiccup people use in the middle of a word, like when you say uh-oh. For example, my friend doesn't say "butter". He says "BU-er". Delicious.

I think glottal stops make a savory stew out of a language that would otherwise be a bland broth. It just adds a certain something that draws you in. And dozens of languages use them.

I also love that click consonant that several African languages use. Sadly, they are starting to disappear. That breaks my heart because they're delightful.

Oh, who am I kidding? I love accents and dialects of every stripe. I can spot a Dutch accent from 50 paces, and it always brings me back to the wonderful summer I spent in Holland. Indian accents make me think of the delectable smells and tastes and rich colors of that country. If you whisper in my ear with a Spanish accent, you have me at hola.

The tonal languages of Asia fascinate me as well, although I'd be afraid to attempt one. I don't have the ear for such things. I can't even tune a guitar.

I can't imagine living a life that is isolated from all the scrumptious differences that this world has to offer. I want to dive into your voice and just bathe there for a while. Would you mind?

Xenophobes don't know what they're missing.

First published on February 16, 2014

If You're Happy and You Know It, Clap Your Hands

*Sometimes it's better to stop questioning and
just let the ear worm invade your brain.*

I woke up humming that song from my childhood the other day. I have no idea why. And then I started thinking about the lyrics. It's been my experience that it's never a good idea to examine the lyrics from childhood too closely. (If you know the true meaning behind Ring Around the Rosie, for example, and you aren't totally creeped out by it, you have no soul.)

But think about it. "If you're happy and you know it"? Are there scenarios in which you could be happy and *not* know it? If so, what a pity. I'd like to always know when I'm happy so I can savor the feeling and appreciate it.

But if there are moments when you are happy and you don't know it, I guess by definition you'd never know that. Which makes you wonder about your awareness in general. Then you have to wonder if there's any way to improve upon that awareness.

Oh, my head hurts.

But I've got you singing that song now, haven't I?

First published on <u>September 16, 2014</u>

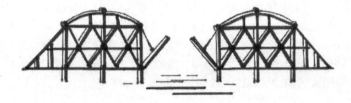

I'm Dating Myself

Appreciate yourself, and actually show it!

I've been in high stress mode for a while now, between the death of my boyfriend, a horrific financial situation, and having to find and then move to another house. I am on the ragged edge. I need a break.

It would be really nice if someone would bring me flowers, take me out to dinner, and then give me a nice foot massage (among other things). I want to be pampered, cared for, and cuddled. I want to be appreciated and accepted and feel special.

Unfortunately, I'm fat and 49 and I work the graveyard shift, so my field of potential suitors is, well, nonexistent. But hold on. *I* care about me. I appreciate and accept me most of the time. Why can't I pamper myself? Why can't I do something special by myself? And why does it never occur to most of us to entertain that option?

So as soon as the dust settles from this move, I intend to take myself out on a date. (I've already asked myself, and I told myself yes.) I'm going to buy myself some flowers. I'm going to splurge on something extravagant to eat. Then I'm going to take myself home, play some smooth jazz, light a candle, turn the lights out, and take a nice bath. Yeah, that's what I'm gonna do. If I play my cards right, I may even take myself to bed. Because I think I'm quite a catch.

First published on July 2, 2014

In Pursuit of the Perseids

There's nothing better than going on an adventure with friends without getting arrested.

"Talking to cops now," she texted.

That's usually not good. We had planned on meeting in a park on the shores of Lake Sammamish after midnight so we could sit and gaze at the sky over the water, without the nuisance of city lights, and enjoy the Perseids meteor shower. Turns out that Redmond's finest don't appreciate random people hanging about in public parks after dark. Even harmless folks like us.

Well, this was awkward. We'd all driven about an hour to reach this destination. Now what?

The officer was kind enough to direct them to a soccer field about 5 miles away, so she texted me the address. And of course I promptly got lost. I wound up in some highly secure facility where the guards wore paramilitary outfits. I was asked to leave.

Good grief, but this is a secure town. Yes, it's the home of Microsoft, but come on. I'm a fat old 50-year-old white chick who just happens to be wandering about after midnight. What kind of shenanigans could I be getting into?

I called her and said I didn't know where the heck I was, and she handed the phone to her boyfriend, who got me headed in the right direction. You'd think with an address and a GPS, I wouldn't have so much difficulty, but I'm of Viking descent, and we managed to lose America, so at least I come by it honestly.

Finally I arrived, and we unloaded the lawn chairs and they loaned me a long sleeved shirt, because, silly Floridian that I am, it didn't occur to me that the temperature actually drops at night in Washington State. I provided the lifesavers. It's always good to have some hard candy sweetness when you're having to be patient. We went to the center of the field, sat down, and gazed expectantly at the sky.

Well, the shower turned out to be a bit more of a sprinkle. Every once in a while, two of us would see a really spectacular one, and the third one, who had been looking elsewhere, would go, "Awww, *man!* Seriously?"

In between meteors, we bantered. And they are as good at that as I am. I laughed so hard I became breathless. And I got to watch a truly loving couple and imagine that maybe somehow, some day, it won't be too late for me to have that. It gave me hope.

So overall, despite nearly being arrested and getting lost, the evening was a huge success, and I will forever cherish the memory. You can't beat spending time with friends.

The next night when I got off work I turned off all my lights, went into my back yard, completely flattened my lawn chair and lay down and gazed upward. My dogs kept coming out to check on me, especially when they'd hear me gasp, which I did frequently. Because that night, in spite of being in the city, I was treated to an amazing display of shooting stars. That was a good night, too.

I can't wait for next year.

First published on <u>*August 14, 2015*</u>

Independence

The 4th of July always causes me to count my blessings in terms of human rights. I have a great deal to be thankful for.

I'm feeling particularly patriotic today, because marriage equality was recently made the law of the land here in the United States. Every once in a while, for all its flaws, this country gets it right. That makes me feel good.

So, one of my traditions on Independence Day is that I take some time to contemplate what independence means to me, as a woman, as an American, as a human being on this planet. And I'm not just talking independence from England, which is what this holiday was originally about.

Every day, all over the world, people experience varying levels of freedom. I happen to think that on that particular bell curve, I'm one of the luckier ones. But even on this day of flag waving and euphoria, I'm not going to say we get everything right. Some of my freedoms have been rolled back over time, and others are constantly being chipped away at. Independence isn't some final destination. It's not like you can sit back and rest once you've arrived. It takes work to maintain.

Here are a few things that I value highly, whether I have them or not:

Coming and going as I please.
Marrying whomever I want, divorcing if I choose, or never marrying at all.

Education.

The right to decide what I can and cannot do with my own body.

Access to health care.

Having no one else dictate what clothes I wear.

Being able to drive a car.

Freely stating my opinions in this blog.

Pursuing my own spiritual path.

Owning my own property.

Voting.

Protesting and debating.

Living alone, or with whomever I choose.

Celebrating differences.

Traveling freely.

Choosing my own career path, or in fact working at all.

Feeling safe.

All of these things, and so many more, are what independence means to me. If you have these things, you are very fortunate indeed. Don't take them for granted. Today, and every other day of the year, we should appreciate what we have and maintain it, and strive for these basic human rights for all.

Happy Independence Day.

First published on July 4, 2015

It Came Without Ribbons

*Standing alone and looking Christmas squarely in the eye,
I Still manage to feel grateful.*

'Twas an odd Christmas indeed for me this year in this land of total strangers. I didn't deck the halls with boughs of holly. I didn't string lights. I didn't attend parties or wrap gifts. I left no cookies out for Santa as I knew that this year he'd pass on by. It's hard to put on the ritz for a party of one. Instead I went to work.

While others donned their ugly Christmas sweaters, I was struggling into a pair of coveralls that make me look like a prison inmate. While others were drinking egg nog and singing carols, I was wiping the grease off trunions. While others were watching It's a Wonderful Life, I was removing grime from buffer landings and striker plates. Drawbridges don't clean themselves, don't you know.

Before you start feeling sorry for me, though, I have to say that I was actually quite happy doing all this, and not just because of the double time and a half pay rate. Although I had been braced to feel completely sorry for myself, somewhere along the way this feeling washed over me. It was the purest, most sincere sense of gratitude I've ever felt in my life. It actually brought sappy little tears of joy to my eyes.

After a couple years of pure hell, it suddenly occurred to me that in actual fact I'm in a really good place in my life right now.

I'm not sure how I lucked out. A lot of it really was total dumb luck. But here I am, reaping the benefits regardless.

I've got the best job I've ever had in my life. I'm living in a really cool city. I've got my dogs, and a nice, safe place to live. I get to sleep at night like a normal person for the first time in 13 years. Things are really quite good. The rest will come.

At some point this made me think of that scene in the Grinch where he realizes that even though he's taken all the material things away from the people of Who-ville, somehow he hasn't managed to steal Christmas. Whether you're a Christian or not, much can be learned from that story. Gratitude and love are what counts in this world. All the rest is just frosting. The cake is the thing.

And I do feel gratitude and I have love in abundance. Life is good.

First published on <u>December 26, 2014</u>

It's Not Easy Being Green

Wrap your differences in a Kermit-the-Frog-like embrace!

The first time I heard Kermit the Frog sing that song when I was a little girl, it made me cry. And I have to admit it still chokes me up to this day. That's because I've felt green my whole life.

In this case, "green" means different from everybody else, and yet somehow not particularly special. I feel green when I hear coworkers getting all enthusiastic because we've got a new hire and "she's gorgeous" (as in, "what a refreshing change.") I feel green when my intellectual friends start speaking computer-ese, and I suddenly feel as though I should be chewing bubble gum. I feel green when I share my unique perspective and am met with blank stares.

In America, we claim to prize individuality, but most people seem to want to be popular and accepted and understood. "Cool" seems to mean trendy, but it has to be trendy enough to where everyone wants to follow that trend. You're expected to stand out in a crowd, but only as a leader of that crowd, not as someone who is on the sidelines, alone.

Boy, Kermit wasn't kidding. It's not easy. Not even a little bit. Sometimes it hurts like hell.

But because I'd start blubbering the minute he started to sing, I seem to have missed the point of the whole song. If you listen to it all the way through, you realize that what Kermit is trying to say is that, yes, it's not easy. But it's important. We all have a role to play. We all matter. We need to accept ourselves and love ourselves for who we are. Because, after all, green is a fundamental part of the color spectrum. This world would be a lot more ugly without green.

First published on <u>May 6, 2015</u>

Knocking on Neighbors' Doors

What delightful diversity there is in this world!

Whenever I move into a new neighborhood, I always think that I should go and introduce myself to my neighbors.

Unfortunately, I never quite get around to it. I'll usually get to know the people right next door (And I'm lucky in that I happen to have fantastic next door neighbors these days), but that's about it. I will wave and smile at people as I drive past them on the street and leave it at that.

I'm shy. I like my privacy. And if I'm honest, I'm rather lazy.

But recently I desperately needed my neighbors' help. My dog ran away. After exhausting all other resources, I was getting desperate. So I printed up a mini-flyer with my dog's picture and my contact information, and I knocked on every single door on my street.

Sometimes people weren't home, so I'd tape the flyer to their door handle and leave. Other times it was quite obvious that they were there, but they refused to come to the door. For Pete's sake, I'm just a fat old lady. I don't pose any threat. But they probably thought I was going to hand them a religious tract or something. Fine. I'd leave my flyer for them, too.

But about half the people did come to the door, and when I'd tell them my story, they'd express sympathy and say they'd keep an eye out. That was a great comfort to me. There are a lot of genuinely decent people on my street.

But what was most intriguing about the process was that I have a completely different view of my neighborhood now. First of all, it's a lot more diverse than I realized. People pretty much keep to themselves. When I took this opportunity to talk to them, I was treated to a variety of accents and couplings and age groups and skin colors. That really delighted me.

And just by standing in their doorways, I was able to draw a great deal of conclusions. They may not be accurate, but they were fascinating. It seems that one family cares for an extremely disabled, wheelchair-bound man. Another couple has adopted or fosters a child of a different race. Love it! Another guy is obviously a very old and rather lonely bachelor. Some people are struggling financially. Others had well-appointed homes. Some had mellow households, others were ruled by chaos.

I came away from these encounters rather impressed with how many different ways there are to live life. I came away feeling like I was part of a larger community. Even though the circumstances weren't ideal, I'm glad I took the time to knock on my neighbors' doors.

(Oh, and by the way, my dog and I were reunited after two of the longest days of my life. Yay!)

First published on <u>March 9, 2016</u>

Lagniappe

*Giving a little something extra to show your gratitude pays
dividends beyond anything you can imagine.*

For those of you who have never been to New Orleans, allow
me to introduce you to the world's most delightful custom:
Lagniappe. This word came to the English language via the
Louisiana French by way of the Spanish Creoles from the
Quechua word yapay. Whew! The fact that it managed to
survive so many cultures to arrive at our door tells you what a
wonderful tradition it is.

Basically it means "a little something extra", like the 13th
doughnut in a baker's dozen. It sort of reminds me of the
obligatory encore that musicians will do at the end of a concert.
Everybody knows it's going to happen, but we're still delighted
when it does. Vendors in New Orleans will throw in a little
something extra with your purchase if you ask. This, to me,
indicates what astute businessmen these people are, because
when I walk away feeling I've gotten a little more for my
money, it makes me want to go back.

Oddly enough, my first experience with Lagniappe occurred in
Asheville, North Carolina at the Open Door Boutique. I bought a
dress there 30 years ago, and they included a stick of incense in
my bag. I was confused, then delighted by this little extra thing.
It made me feel appreciated. So appreciated, in fact, that I have
remembered the experience for decades. And it probably didn't
cost them more than a few pennies. I'm sure I've bought things
from small boutiques a hundred times in my life, but this is the

only shop whose name I remember. (They're still open by the way, but I have no idea if they still practice Lagniappe. I hope they do.)

So, for all you shop owners out there, take heed: this tiny little investment in your customers will bring you a lifetime of loyalty, and that's worth its weight in gold.

So here is my lagniappe for you, dear reader: something to think about.

"Calm seas do not an expert sailor make." –Unknown

First published on June 23, 2013

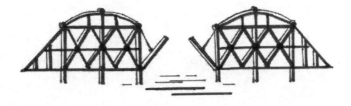

Learning your Lessons

Ah, there's nothing quite like the gift of learning your lesson.

Every one of us has certain lessons to learn throughout his or her life. Some lessons we are doomed to repeat over and over again. Other lessons impact us on such fundamental levels that it only takes one time to get the message. It doesn't always feel very good when we get schooled, but like it or not, it's always a valuable experience.

Learning from our mistakes when we are young can be particularly humiliating. We are already in a phase in which we feel we know it all and are utterly self-conscious about the ways we are perceived by others, so when we receive a moral or ethical smack-down it particularly stings. In hindsight one can accept that lessons learned when young are the most valuable of all because we benefit from them for the rest of our lives, but at the time it feels as if it's an exercise in torture.

Here's a lesson I learned when young. Friends who are cruel to others will eventually direct their cruelty toward you as well. It might be fun in high school when there are cliques and insecurities and pecking orders are being established with a vengeance, but in the wider world, bullies are less accepted and can be even more destructive.

Take a stand and defend those who are being attacked. Do not tolerate aggressive people. Pit Bulls turn on their masters every day.

Take a moment to appreciate the lessons you have learned in life. They have made you a much better person. They are gifts.

First published on June 27, 2013

Life Begins at 50

I have no idea if 50 is the new 30, but it definitely has been a new start, and that has been an unexpected gift.

I've spent much of my life fearing the passage of time. I wasn't obsessed with the topic, but I didn't want to get older, that was for sure. What a waste of energy that fear was.

First of all, aging is inevitable. All the plastic surgery and vitamins and exercise in the world isn't going to stop it. We all have an expiration date. (And thank goodness for that! The planet is crowded enough.)

But here's what kind of took me by surprise: I like myself a lot more than I did at 19. Granted, I wouldn't mind having my 19-year-old body back, but if I had to be the person I was at 19 to achieve that goal, I'd turn down the offer.

At 19 I was on a hormonal roller coaster. I was desperate to be liked, and really concerned about what other people thought. I didn't know where my life was going, and spent a lot of time comparing my insides to other people's outsides. I wasted a lot of energy dwelling on how unfair life was, and trying really hard to get... where, exactly? What, exactly? I had no idea. All I knew was that things were supposed to be much, much better than they were. I don't know where the ruler came from that I was using to measure my life, but I knew I was falling short, and therefore I was pretty miserable for the most part.

And then a funny thing happened. As I got older, I made a lot more mistakes. I learned a lot more lessons. I had a lot more experiences, and accumulated a lot more memories. And I came to realize that not only am I the sum total of all that stuff, but also I still have so much to look forward to! I now know that I'll never be able to predict the path my life will take, but now that excites me.

Bring it on!

First published on <u>August 18, 2015</u>

Life is for Learning-

Be a sponge. Soak up knowledge! It's free! What a gift!

Someone said to me recently, "Life is for learning." Very true, my friend. The common thread that flows through every life experience is the opportunity to increase your knowledge, should you choose to accept it.

The ability to absorb information– what a gift! Even if it's just your basic, "Maybe I should never stick my hand in a fire again," it is more valuable than gold. On a fundamental level it is how we survive. Even plants know to turn toward the sun. As we grow more sophisticated, it helps us strive to become our highest self.

There are people out there who take a hostile stance when it comes to knowledge. They try to make intellectual a dirty word. They don't want you to think, or worse, they prefer to tell you what to think.

In the spiritual realm, these include those religious groups that strongly discourage you from questioning anything. They give you a very clear cut set of beliefs, and they expect you to strictly adhere to their dogma. Your compliance will make you one of the chosen ones. Any deviation relegates you to an eternity of suffering of one form or another. To these people I say that we were given a brain, so I assume we were expected to use it.

In politics, ignorance seems to be the default position these days, but especially avoid those parties that want to keep you in a state of fear. Fear makes you easy to manipulate. But the more you know about something, the less you fear it. So it is in their best interest to get you to turn away from knowledge. They especially hate science. Heaven forfend we believe the results of reasoned research! That might mean we have to *do* something! Much easier to bury our heads in the sand and maintain the status quo. (The status quo that they want to maintain, anyway.)

In relationships, the most toxic ones are those where your partner expects you to shut up and do what you're told. They are the men who want to keep the little woman at home, and the women, too, who rule with an iron fist. Also avoid those people who are so comfortable in their routines that if a loved one wants to take up a new interest, they strongly discourage it. A truly loving individual will not only delight when you spread your wings, but he or she will help you to fly.

Grab every opportunity to learn. Value education, but also take something away from every experience you have, even the negative ones. They, too, have something to teach you. Every person who crosses your path is a teacher as well. Actively pursue knowledge. Be a sponge. Read everything you can get your hands on. Exercise your curiosity. Stick your head below the surface, but don't leave it in the sand.

Seek. Inquire. Delve. Share. Expand. Take advantage of this gift we have been given, and question any person or group that attempts to discourage you from doing so. Knowledge really is power.

First published on June 2, 2014

Life is Like a Bowl of Pho

Lessons can spring forth from inanimate objects.
Especially the delicious ones.

First of all, if you've never had pho, that Vietnamese delicacy, the soup of soups, the comfort food of all time, then stop reading this right now and go get some. Drive for 4 hours if you need to. Slap your mama if she stands in your way. Seriously. What are you waiting for? Go! Go! Go! You haven't lived until you've had pho. And for the love of God, when you order it, pronounce it properly. Call it "fuh", not "foe".

Having said that, and since I have just come home from a delightful evening of pure pho indulgence which has warmed the very cockles of my heart, I feel I have earned the right to wax philosophical, so here is my theory: Life is like a bowl of pho.

The rice noodles are long and tangled and look deceptively unappetizing, but once you dive in, you find that you love the experience. It may be a bit messy, and it may not portray you at your most attractive, but after a time you will find that you don't care. You're too busy basking in the experience to notice the reactions of others.

And the broth, good heavens, the broth! It looks simple and clear, but it is such a sophisticated taste sensation that you know you'd give anything to reproduce it at home, but you're most likely never going to make the attempt because, surely, if it's that delicious, it must take so much effort and efficiency that you'll fear you lack the ability.

The most delightful thing about pho, as with life, is that no two people will ever have the same experience. Not only can you choose pho beef or chicken or brisket or meatballs or tripe or...you name it, but the restaurant wait staff will provide you with a variety of items that you may add to your soup. Lime, mint leaves, cilantro, bean sprouts, Thai Basil, chili peppers, a variety of sauces, each one hotter than the next. Some people prefer their pho to be spicy. I myself am not a party animal. I stay out of the clubs in life, and I don't drown my pho in chili sauce. Even so, pho is the first thing I crave when I have a cold or when it's cold outside.

Pho provides you with a great deal of choices—not only the garnishes mentioned above, but also how to eat it. Are you talented or brave? Then go for the chopsticks. Are you more pragmatic? Would you rather make the most of your ability to consume? Do you not care if your actions fly in the face of impressing your dining companion? Then ask for a fork.

I'm a fork girl, myself, but I also believe in living life to the fullest, so I will give you one very important piece of advice. In pho and in life, order extra, because the second half gets even better.

Sigh. Now I've gone and made myself hungry. I don't think those leftovers will make it to lunchtime.

First published on December 27, 2012

Danish Hygge

I am forever grateful for my Danish heritage, because it influenced me greatly growing up. It accounts for a great deal of who I have become.

Perhaps it's some long lost cultural memory implanted in my psyche, or maybe it's just a normal part of being human, but I love to get all cozy. I like warm fuzzy slippers and evenings by the fire with friends. I like snuggling with my dogs in a warm bed when it's raw and wet outside. I like getting lost deep in the stacks of my public library, surrounded by exciting dusty books, knowing that no one knows where I am. I like sitting around a campfire with a group of delightful people.

The Danes actually have a word for it: *Hygge* (pronounced hooglie), it is a very important part of their culture. I am ½ Danish, so I may come by this genetically. I have to say that any group that has a word for this feeling, cozy yet social, warm, cuddly, inviting... that is a group that I'm proud to be a part of.

Hav en hyggelig dag!

First published on <u>November 4, 2014</u>

Looking Forward

My idea of hell would be having nothing to anticipate.

Sometime in the next few days I'll be taking a ferry from Seattle out to <u>Port Townsend</u>, and I'm so excited. I've been itching to explore the surrounding area for quite some time, and Port Townsend is said to be an artsy little Victorian seaport. One of my coworkers even says there's a beach near there comprised entirely of sea glass. I can't wait to see that. I have no doubt that I'll be blogging about it!

I'll be staying with a new friend and her parents. It will be a rare treat for me to have that much human contact. They seem like amazing people.

Then, about a month after that, I'll be going to <u>Yellowstone National Park</u> with my sister and brother-in-law and an unbelievable menagerie of our pets. I've been to Yellowstone before, and there's no place like it. I'm looking forward to seeing how my dogs react to a bison. (From an extremely safe distance, of course.)

It occurs to me that it's a delicious experience, having things to look forward to. I highly recommend it. I also enjoy living for the moment, although I find that to be difficult sometimes. Anything that keeps me from dwelling on the past or brooding over stressful stuff is quite welcome. I do tend to brood.

I am prone to depression, but I've found that I can sort of skip over the top of it like a stone skipping over water if I can hop from one "Looking Forward To" event to the next. My idea of hell is having nothing to anticipate. And being in that state is entirely under your control.

Don't just sit there! Make plans! It doesn't have to be elaborate or expensive. I'm looking forward to making Toad in the Hole for dinner tonight, for example.

So get curious! Explore. Create. Do.

First published on August 1, 2015

Barb Abelhauser

March Forth!

The 4th of March should be celebrated every year.

Today is the only date in the entire year that constitutes a grammatically correct sentence when spoken aloud. March fourth. March forth!

That's a call to action; a day to get off the couch and do something. It should be a holiday.

Carpe diem! Seize the day! A rolling stone gathers no moss! Don't put off for tomorrow what you can do today! Just do it! You only live once! Life is short!

A friend of mine who has died and been revived several times likes to say, "You have been given a perfectly good day. What will you do with it?"

First published on <u>March 4, 2014</u>

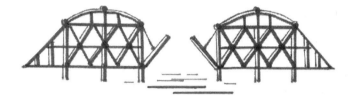

Mindfulness

Breathe in. Breathe out. You're here right now. Isn't it great?

According to Psychology Today, "Mindfulness is a state of active, open attention to the present. When you're mindful, you observe your thoughts and feelings from a distance, without judging them good or bad. Instead of letting your life pass you by, mindfulness means living in the moment and awakening to experience."

I have to admit that I suck at this. I don't even have the patience to attempt meditation. I'm too busy planning and organizing and making contingencies for anticipated disaster. I suppose this comes from a lifetime of being the only one in my boat. If I don't steer this thing, who will?

But every once in a while, through no effort of my own, I get a brief, shining moment of mindfulness. I'll look about me and realize that this moment, right now, is perfect in every way, even if there are flaws. The light glinting off the water, the tangy bite of citrus, the people I'm with... all somehow combine to make me realize that I wouldn't want to be anywhere else on earth.

Everything seems to fall into place in times like these. I'm convinced that it's these moments that will flash before my eyes when I celebrate my life on my way to the next state of being. Whatever that may be.

Anyone who regularly practices mindfulness is a fortunate person indeed. I'm working on it. I'll probably never achieve perfection in this realm.

But even having just a few seconds of it now and again in a lifetime is a precious gift.

First published on <u>*December 7, 2015*</u>

My Crunchy Granola Epiphany

Welcome to the REAL world wide web!

Last night at about 4 a.m., alone at work and struggling to stay awake, I had an epiphany, and now I'm looking at the world in an entirely different way. Before I present you with my concept, let me say that I'm quite sure this theory didn't originate with me. There are plenty of crunchy granola new-agey types out there who no doubt have come to the same or similar conclusions. And how's this for a revelation: my philosophy doesn't even have to be true for it to have a positive impact on me. Awesome.

I'm calling it Net Theory, and it's deceptively simple: Everything is connected. All of us are one. From what little I understand about Quantum Theory, I'm fairly certain that it supports this notion. On a sub-atomic level, we're all a part of one big, uh....thing. We're bathing in a sea of light waves. There is really no place where I end and you begin.

And once you accept this idea, the way you perceive the universe changes. For example, I'm not as irritated by obnoxious people. I'm just grateful that they are performing this role instead of me. I'm not jealous of people who are more successful than I am, because their success is a reflection of the healthy part of this great net. Politics seem even sillier if that's possible. It's just one side of us disagreeing with the other side of us, and whoever comes out on top, well, it's still us. Prejudice seems absurd, as does war, violence, cruelty, selfishness, pollution, road rage, even petty grudges, because it's all negative energy directed at the great net of which we are all a part. In other words, it's self-destructive. I suspect that moving forward, I won't be as bothered by boredom, because I'll know that somewhere something interesting is happening. I won't resent work, because it's part of what needs to be done.

Charity will seem like a way to be good to myself, as will sex and learning. Religion makes much more sense, because it seems like someone must be keeping this massive organism, for lack of a better word, on track.

Eating, I was musing on the way in to work tonight, is kind of problematic. Am I eating myself? Yuck! But then, why not? It is the gift I give to myself to maintain life. That's actually beautiful, if you ask me. It's kind of like the last supper writ large. (It sure makes me want to avoid junk food, though.)

And the more I get into this concept, the less I am afraid of dying, because now more than ever I can believe that I'll still be a part of this great interconnectedness that is all of us and everything. I can't imagine anything more comforting than that.

First published on <u>February 13, 2013</u>

My Own Personal Garden Song

One step at a time. Inch by inch, you'll get there.

After pulling up stakes and moving 3100 miles across country to a place where I know no one, essentially starting over at age 50, I spent a lot of time beating myself up because upon arrival I didn't instantly have it all figured out.

I don't know what I was thinking. Was everything supposed to fall into place, as if I could just pick up where I left off in Florida, like the new job and the new place to live and the cross-country jaunt were mere hiccups in my day-to-day routine? Reinventing yourself isn't for sissies, let me tell you.

Fast forward 6 months, and yes, I love where I'm living. I've even more than halfway unpacked. I love 95 percent of my job, and I actually go long periods of time not dwelling on the other 5 percent. I've even started to establish a stable, albeit quirky, routine. And I can now go several places, like the library and the grocery store and to work, without relying on my GPS, which is nice.

But yeah, I admit it. I haven't made a single friend outside of work yet, and that sucks. I'm lonely. And before you even go there, I've been given a million suggestions about how to rectify that. If I pursued them all I'd probably be so popular that I'd have to change my phone number just to get some peace. So I feel kind of guilty. I should be on top of things. I have all the tools. And yet, here I am, alone.

But today I started humming the Arlo Guthrie version of the Garden Song, which has also been famously sung by John Denver; Pete Seeger; and Peter, Paul, and Mary to name a few. You know the song. It starts, "Inch by inch, row by row, I'm gonna make this garden grow. All it takes is a rake and a hoe and a piece of fertile ground..."

And I suddenly realized that what I'm doing is transplanting my life. I uprooted myself from Florida and I'm putting down roots here. That's going to take some time and patience, some love and care. I just need to go inch by inch. I don't have to beat myself up when, at the end of the day, the whole darned garden isn't planted and in full bloom.

I need to give myself a break, do things correctly and with positive intention, and it will all work out in the end. Yes, I have the rake and the hoe. I'll get there.

Next stop for me is signing up for a pottery class at the nearby community college. That starts in April. I'm looking forward to it. And I'm sure I'll meet some amazing people.

Forward motion is what counts. Even if it's only an inch at a time.

First published on _March 9, 2015_

Barb Abelhauser

My Prayer

If there were ever something that I've written that
I should start off each day repeating, this is it.

I am grateful this day for the rain that sustains me
for the sun that nurtures me, for the wind that buffets me.
I wish to give back more than I take from this world,
value more than that which is has been given me
and shore up that which has always endured me.
May I always gaze at the stars and feel joy
for my minuscule part in the limitless universe.

First published on July 13, 2013

My Sister's Apple Pie

There are some ingredients in life for which
there are no substitutes.

My sister does not fancy herself to be a good cook. I couldn't tell you, really, as I haven't eaten many of her meals in years. But I will say this: she makes the best apple pie on the face of the earth.

I have no idea how she does it. It's not like she has kept the recipe a secret from me. I've tried it, and I just can't seem to replicate it despite all my efforts. It's just not the same.

And now that we live on opposite sides of the country, I suspect that I may go years between pies. That's tragic. But I can't imagine apple pie would ship well, so it's one of the many sacrifices I didn't consider when I decided to relocate. If I had, I might still be on the East coast.

In retrospect, I think I know the one ingredient that I'm unable to add when trying to make my sister's pie. My sister. She's what makes it so delicious. I'm very lucky to have her in my world, even at a distance.

First published on December 28, 2015

Nostomania

I don't feel homesick after all! Yay, me!

From dictionary.reference.com:
nostomania
[nos-tuh–mey-nee-uh, –meyn-yuh]
noun
1. intense homesickness; an irresistible compulsion to return home.

I love words. That's why I'm a blogger.

This one strikes a particular chord with me because I have recently moved 3100 miles across the country. But am I homesick? Not really. To be homesick you have to first feel like you had a home, and I haven't really had that feeling in many years.

There is a related word, though.
nostalgia
[no-stal-juh, -jee-uh, nuh-]
noun
1. a wistful desire to return in thought or in fact to a former time in one's life.

Do I feel nostalgia? Definitely. I miss Popeye's Chicken, sunshine, manatee, and friends (not necessarily in that order). I miss being a home owner. I miss good, inexpensive tomatoes and knowing my way around without using a GPS. I miss driving past places that spark memories within me.

Fond memories I have. A longing to go back, I don't. Go back to what? There's nothing to go back to. So I guess I'm not a Nostomaniac. I'm just a sentimental old fool.

First published on <u>November 29, 2014</u>

On Being Busy

Being thrust into the fast lane when you've spent most of your time rambling along the country roads feels exceedingly strange.

Ever since <u>StoryCorps</u> contacted me and told me they wanted to include my 2009 interview in their anthology <u>Callings</u>, and oh, by the way, NPR wants to feature you in <u>Morning Edition</u>, and <u>Parade Magazine</u> wants to do a piece on you as well, and O Magazine would like to speak with you, and wouldn't you like to start publishing anthologies of your own? And would you be my first podcast interview for <u>Shaping Sapiens</u>? And can I link to your blog? And maybe you should create a <u>Facebook Group</u> for your blog. Ever since all these things have happened, I've been busy.

And when I say "busy", I mean it feels like someone has taped a rocket to my behind and I have absolutely no control over the steering. I'm not used to this. Not at all.

For over 14 years I've been locked away on my little drawbridge, enjoying relative peace and quiet, with very few ducks to put into very short rows. And I've liked it that way. Now, there are deadlines and decisions and attention and... I can't believe this is all happening.

Is it exciting? God, yes! But it feels as if time is moving so fast that I might not be able to keep up. It makes me nervous.

My writing has been all about stopping and looking closely at things. It's been about watching and commenting from the background. A friend calls me a professional meditator, a grand observer. I worry that I'm losing some of that in all this kerfuffle.

But I intend to ride the crest of this wave for as long as it lasts and savor every minute of it! Of course it isn't going to last forever. Yes, I'll miss it when it's gone. But I think I'll also be kind of relieved when everything slows back down and settles into a nice little routine once more.

I've been told it takes a special kind of person to sit still for 40 hours a week and not go crazy. I guess I'm that person. I thrive on it. But it is rather thrilling to go out and salsa in this world every now and then!

First published on <u>April 22, 2016</u>

On Making a Fool of Oneself

Sometimes you just have to act silly.

I just watched a short <u>Youtube video</u> about a guy in Perth, Australia who likes to start impromptu dance parties with strangers on trains. What fun! Before long, most everyone on the train is getting their groove on, and I'm sure they all have smiles on their faces for the rest of the day.

I am a big proponent of making a fool of oneself. That doesn't mean it's within my comfort zone to do so, but I've found that when I give myself that extra little push and do something silly...Wow! What a rush. It's liberating.

I did notice one guy on that train who wouldn't dance, and sat there frowning. I know a lot of people like that. They absolutely will not play under any circumstances. They tend to be bitter, angry people that are filled with regrets. I feel sorry for them.

But I don't feel so sorry for them that I wouldn't boogie down. Life's too short!

First published on <u>May 12, 2015</u>

On Staying Put

*On reflection, it occurs to me that it's a wonderful thing
to be able to learn from one's mistakes.*

The worst mistake I've ever made was staying for decades in a
situation that made me unhappy. I now look back on those
years with sadness and wonder what I could have achieved if I
only had the courage to listen to my gut. But no. I played it safe.
I didn't want to hurt anyone's feelings. I thought that by putting
everyone's needs ahead of my own, I was being a good person.
The truth was that I was afraid to take risks. What a massive
waste.

In essence I held myself back, and by extension I'm pretty sure
I held everyone around me back as well. I thought I was being
kind by not rocking their boats, but actually I was being selfish.
By not allowing myself to grow, I was stunting the growth of
the people I cared about most.

Now that I've started leaning toward my growing edge, I've
discovered that I've made a positive impact on a lot of people
without even trying. I've been told that by doing my thing and
living my joy, I've influenced others to take chances. I've gotten
people moving and applying for jobs, and actually taking their
talents seriously. I've encouraged people out of toxic
relationships. I've introduced people who would otherwise
have never known each other, and that's sparked some
amazing collaborations. I've shown people different ways to
look at the world. I feel as though I've opened some sort of

flood gate and the abundance therefrom is washing over more than just me.

Am I taking credit for other people's lives and choices? No. Of course not. Life is way too complex for that. But I have to say that I'm noticing this existential shift all around me, and I don't think I'd be seeing it, feeling it, or experiencing it if I had simply stayed put. I had to get into the flow to be a part of it, to increase that flow.

The worst thing you can do is make choices for yourself based on how others might feel or react. Doing so assumes that their present existence is their best existence. That means you are underestimating them. You have no idea how your changes might free them up to make changes of their own.

So don't stay put. Don't cling. Don't become stagnant. Move! Grow! There's a big old world all around you. Experience it!

First published on July 3, 2016

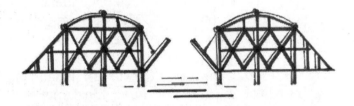

Operation Sack Lunch

I went there to give, but I got back even more.

It was nearly 1 o'clock, and people were already starting to line up across the street from Seattle Municipal Tower, arguably the main hub of administration and influence in the city. These people in line, however, had no power or influence. In fact, most of polite society tries desperately to ignore their existence.

They are what the tactless and uncharitable might call the dregs of society; the homeless, the mentally ill, the drug addicted, the working poor, the financially destitute. They are the hungry who have no means of supporting their nasty food habit. This continual need for nutrition is the great equalizer.

I'd be lying if I said I didn't approach this crowd with a certain level of trepidation. You're taught from childhood not to talk to strangers, especially smelly, scary, unpredictable ones. But approach them I did. I was part of a group of coworkers who had volunteered with <u>Operation Sack Lunch</u> to serve that day's midday meal.

Operation Sack Lunch is an amazing Seattle organization. They serve three meals a day, seven days a week, every single day of the year. Free to all comers, no questions asked. According to their website, in 2015 they served 435,711 meals to almost 10,000 individuals at 18 locations in the city. From those stats, it's easy to see that without their help, many people would have starved to death, here in the heart of one of the most prosperous cities in the most prosperous nation in the world.

On this day, like so many other Pacific Northwest days, it was cold and the rain was pouring down. We were all grateful for the steady, loud hum of cars on the interstate overpass above our heads. And yet the people came from all directions, about 270 of them that day, to face our volunteer force of ten. They formed a polite line.

The meal was simple but nutritious: rice, salad, salmon patties, a drink. We were all given a task to perform. Mine was to pass out sporks, those plastic half spoon/half forks that I've always considered to be one of the handiest inventions of the modern world. That also meant I was their first point of contact in the food line.

At first I was overwhelmed with this steady flow of unrelenting need. I felt inadequate and helpless, and rather pathetic, if I'm honest. Here was privation on a grand scale, and I was handing it a plastic spork. I couldn't meet their eyes.

But they took the high road. Every last one of them, and I mean, every *single* one, thanked me for that spork. I should have responded, "Thank you for understanding that a spork is all I can give you. Today."

And then I began to realize that I could give them something else, however humble: dignity. Courtesy. Respect. So I made myself look each one in the eye and smile and say, "You're welcome." I even joked with a few.

Seeing the women in line was hardest for me to take, somehow. These are dangerous streets. They have to be tough as nails, but they are still at a disadvantage. How do they survive?

This experience had an added layer of angst for me. As I've written a previous blog entry, my late boyfriend, for various and complex reasons, was often mistaken for a homeless person. And sure enough, as I expected would happen, midway down the line was a man that could have been his twin. And strangely enough, he winked at me. He was the only one who winked at me. Why did it have to be *that* guy? I swallowed the grapefruit sized lump in my throat and did my best not to lose it. The hunger of these people was more urgent than my longstanding grief.

There was no pushing, no shoving. Those coming back for seconds waited patiently until everyone got their firsts. And then before I knew it, it was over and the crowd rapidly dispersed. What had been a place of give and take quickly converted itself into a deserted, fenced in patch of parking lot, inhabited by only pigeons and graffiti.

I walked away feeling equal measures of sadness and restored faith in humanity. I was reminded of something that John Bradford said in the 16th century that remains equally true today: "There but for the grace of God go I."

First published on January 26, 2016

Owls and Letters

*There is nothing on earth that's more exciting
than not knowing what's coming your way!*

The owls are going absolutely nuts tonight. There must be ten of them out there, hooting their feathery butts off, and it's been going on for hours. I felt the need to escort my little dogs on their evening backyard bathroom foray for fear they'd be spirited away.

I mentioned this to a friend, who decided to channel J.K. Rowling and say, "Perhaps those owls are bringing you the same letter you haven't been getting all these years…"

And that made me feel excited. Not that I'm anticipating a letter-bearing bird of prey, mind you. But it made me suddenly realize how thin the veil is between me and…potential, I suppose. Something amazing could be just around the corner!

I really *need* something amazing to be just around the corner.

And suddenly the owls are quiet. Too quiet.

First published on <u>August 13, 2013</u>

Pennies in the Parking Lot

*Creating your own family traditions can be
the most intense form of bonding there is.*

A friend and coworker told me a delightful story the other day.
When he has spare change he drops it in parking lots. Why?

When one of his daughters was young, he noticed that she had
inherited his extreme ability to quickly spot when things were
out of place. This ability meant they both always noticed when
there were coins on the ground.

Over time they got into the habit of collecting those coins in a
special jar, and when they got enough money they'd have a
father/daughter outing, such as going to see the movie
Pocahontas or getting ice cream at the mall.

Now that she's grown up and moved away, they naturally don't
do this anymore. So now he drops coins in parking lots because
he figures somewhere out there is another father and daughter
who have taken up the torch and he wants to contribute.

He never mentioned to his daughter that he does this until just
the other day, and she laughed and told him she does the exact
same thing.

So there you have it. This ritual connects them to this day.

And, I suspect this tradition will get passed down through
generations of his family, because I can't imagine a sweeter or

more delightful way to say, "I love you just the way you are and I want to spend time with you."

Stories like this make me wish I had known what it was like to have a father. For those of you who have one, remember that it's never too late to start a new tradition.

First published on June 15, 2014

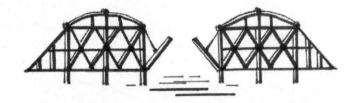

Random Thankfulness

Originally I wrote this one for Thanksgiving,
but it's important to count your blessings
every chance you get.

In spite of an annoying tendency to feel sorry for myself for the past few years, I really do realize that I'm quite lucky, relatively speaking. So here is a list of things that I'm thankful for. It's not all inclusive, of course, and by no means is it in order of importance.

My dogs, who have always given me a reason to tie a knot and hang on when I was at the end of my rope.
Pizza delivery.
An employer who has been willing to re-hire me twice.
Hot water.
My intelligence. The thing I'm most confident about in life is that I'm capable of learning anything if I put my mind to it.
Seasons.
A car that usually starts.
Chocolate.
The roof over my head. I may not really be able to afford it, it may not be where I want it to be, but it keeps the rain off.
Sex.
Sunrises, sunsets and rainbows.
Immunizations.
My closest friends, who have always helped me keep things in perspective.
This blog.
Natural beauty.

The internet.
My government. It may be increasingly screwed up and insane, but I can be fairly confident that there won't be a military coup, that the highways will stay paved, and that no civil war is imminent. Not everyone can be so sure of these things.
Train whistles and fog horns.
Public television and public radio.
My sister, who will always have my back, as I have hers.
Air conditioning.
The fact that I have never once in my life gone to bed hungry.
Art.

I'm grateful for these things not just today, but all year 'round.

First published on <u>November 28, 2013</u>

Roots

Your roots may not run deep or spread wide,
but they can still sustain you.

If things go as planned I'm about to uproot myself and move
3100 miles across the country to a place I've never been, where
I know no one. That's pretty radical, I suppose. But my roots
have never been deep.

I have always sort of envied people with deep roots. People
who go home for the holidays and sleep in their childhood
bedrooms. People who graduate with friends that they played
with in kindergarten

But that's only enviable if they had good childhoods to begin
with. And as we all know, life does not come with that
guarantee. Deep roots are only enviable if the soil that they are
in is optimal.

And being nomadic has its plus sides, too. I've probably been
exposed to more cultures and lifestyles and points of view than
the average person. I also have more options. Rather than eat
"the usual", as delicious as it may be, I prefer to pig out at the
all you can eat buffet.

My roots may not be deep, but they are hardy, and they thrive
in a wide variety of climates. Does that make me a weed? Sure.
Why not. Let's face it: the weeds usually outlast the lawn
anyway.

First published on August 1, 2014

Scars

Even scars can have a silver lining!

After my recent surgery I spent a week in a cast, wondering what my scar was going to look like. I didn't look while the procedure was in progress. I'd have passed out cold.

I needn't have worried, because upon removing the cast I discovered the incision was less than a half inch long, and right where my skin naturally creases, so I suspect that eventually no one will even notice it but me. More shocking was the huge green bruise on my wrist and palm, but that will fade with time.

I actually love scars. On other people. Scars usually come with really interesting stories. They are evidence of a life well-lived. They make people seem more human, somehow.

I remember sitting in a mall as a teenager, and an absolutely mind-blowingly handsome guy walked by. I was in awe. And then he turned his head, and the entire other side of his face was severely, irretrievably burned. It brought tears to my eyes. Not because of the dreadful sight, or what the poor man had obviously been through, but because he'll probably go through his life never knowing how gorgeous he is. That broke my heart. If I had been older and more confident, I might have told him so. I wish I had.

I was talking to a friend the other day about scars. He mentioned that we have a word for the hardening, toughening of skin. Scarring. But we don't have a word for the softening, the opening up, the making more vulnerable.

"Yes we do," I said. "Healing."

First published on July 28, 2015

Self-Care

Be kind to yourself. You deserve it.

For some reason it's been my experience that most people are incapable of being kind to themselves. I'm no exception. I don't know if it's low self-worth or a time management issue, but we tend not to take care of ourselves the way we would others. Think about it. You'd hold a door open for a stranger before you'd hold a figurative door open for yourself, wouldn't you? That's a tragedy.

In this economy especially, it is a shame that we are not taking more opportunities to be kind to ourselves. It costs nothing or next to nothing to allow yourself to sleep in or take a bath instead of a shower. When's the last time you put lotion on your feet or took a walk in a park? Go ahead, splurge on that higher-end ice cream that you love so much, just this once. The dishes can wait. Instead, indulge your desire to watch a few episodes of Star Trek. Or take your bike out of mothballs and go for a ride. What's it going to hurt? Start taking yoga classes again. You know you loved it. Why did you ever stop?

When you've experienced trauma, loss, or illness it is especially important to treat yourself with decency and care. You are the one person you can count on to do that, so why deprive yourself of it? It is wonderful when others step up and are good to you, but you have identified the need and you are also capable of fulfilling it yourself. What's holding you back?

So take an extra few minutes to dangle your feet in the pond or look up at the trees from a hammock or use that shower gel that you like so much. Light that candle. You love the smell. These are gifts you can only give yourself. And when you do, be sure and thank yourself, too. That's another thing we often forget to do, but it's common courtesy.

First published on <u>April 27, 2014</u>

Self-Deprecation -- Your Brain Hears You

Insulting yourself is no joke.

I have this theory. There's a part of your brain that takes in what you hear and assumes it to be fact. My theory is that that goes double for what it hears coming out of your own mouth. Sure, what you say is generated by your brain, but the choice to actually say it is kind of a form of validation. In other words, if you can't trust yourself, who can you trust?

For some reason many of us think it's charming to be self-deprecating. But I'm telling you, your brain hears you when you put yourself down. You might be laughing as you say, "I'm so stupid," or "Women are just not into me," but a little part of your head is just hearing the words and taking them in as reality. In the long run, that is going to hurt you.

We are often more cruel to ourselves than we would ever be to others. That's not funny. That's not charming. It's just wrong. Self-abuse is still abuse. Why don't you deserve as much courtesy and kindness as you would afford a loved one, a guest, or a stranger in distress? You can, should, and MUST become your own cheerleader!

That's my theory for the day.

First published on January 8, 2016

Sentence Envy

I just love being in awe of friends!

As a writer, my ears always prick up when I hear a pithy word combination or an elegant turn of phrase. All these droll fragments get stored in my mental treasure chest, to be trotted out on this blog when the spirit moves me. My thoughts may be original to me, but the way I express them is often a mish-mash of things I've heard from so many places that I couldn't possibly tell you their origins.

It's a little harder to do that with entire sentences, though, without having to own up to downright plagiarism. Take this sentence that I read in a story written by my friend Paul Currington, the leader of the monthly storytelling group I attend called <u>Fresh Ground Stories</u>: "In the coal mine of life my canary is always dead."

I just have to say, it's a rare sentence that makes me roll back my chair and exclaim out loud. "Dang! That's good!" Okay, so I might have punctuated it differently, but that's just my pea-green jealousy talking.

That sentence is a thing of beauty. I'm in love with that sentence. I would have sex with that sentence if I could. Dammit, why didn't *I* think of it?

Moments like this are rather bittersweet. I will always remember that sentence, and how it made me feel when my eyes touched it, but in good conscience I'll never be able to use it.

That's like being treated to the best gelato on earth, but being told you only get to have it once. Given that option, it would take me quite some time to decide if it was worth it, if it meant a lifetime of depravation. (But yeah, in the end I'd have it. I know me.)

I will admit that I've also written a few really good sentences in my life. My favorite one comes from a post that will most likely never be in a future anthology--but the sentence makes me smile:

"Barack Obama eats boysenberry aspic on melba toast while doing the Watusi in a frothy silk kimono."

First published on June 9, 2016

Shakti

A little self-care can go a long way.

I was whining to a friend the other day about how completely and utterly low and defeated I feel. Half of it has to do with this cold or sinus infection or whatever it is that I have. The other half is that I'm coping with losses on just about every front. I feel as if I have been dropped from someplace high. I'm broken in several places and I know it will take years to recover, and I am not entirely sure I have the strength for it. I feel weak and damaged and all settled down on the bottom of the pond, amongst the slime. Bleh. I'm done.

"You need some Shakti," my friend said.

Huh? I have only heard of Shakti mentioned in connection with the Hindu religion, and even in that context I am woefully ignorant of the details.

"Life force," he explained. "Fruit. Vegetables. The fresher the better. Don't you feel better when you eat those things rather than junk food?"

Well, this was a new one, but he did have a point. I do feel better when I eat healthier, and since everything else in my life seems to be completely out of my control, why not? So I had a salad.

And I did feel a little better. Just performing that one act of self-care made the difference. Were all my problems solved? Not even close. But I felt a tiny bit better. Enough to carry on for a few minutes more. And that's enough.

Eat your vegetables.

First published on April 9, 2014

Shovel Friends

The best friends will always help you shovel.

My mother used to say that you can't pick your relatives, but you can pick your friends. And among your many friends, there are always a few who stand head and shoulders above the rest. I call these "shovel friends" because they are the kind you can call up at three in the morning and say, "Meet me in Central Park, and bring a shovel," and they'd be there, because they're that loyal, and they know you so well that they'd be confident that you aren't involved in something that will send them to the state penitentiary.

I can't take credit for originating this concept. I think I heard it on some reality show. But, hey, it resonates with me, and I'm not above stealing a really good idea.

I'm actually lucky enough to have several shovel friends, and they're worth their weight in gold. They have been there for me through my highs and lows, and I have no doubt that they will be there for all my future emotional topography. But make no mistake: shovel friends aren't, and shouldn't be, *blindly* loyal. In fact, a true friend is one who will call you on your stuff. He or she won't let you get away with silliness or stupidity, and will expect mutual respect. These friends can always be counted upon to give you the reality check that you so desperately need. The best friends are the ones who question you and challenge you.

So take a moment to tell your shovel friends how much they mean to you, because they will most likely be the most valuable relationships you'll ever have.

First published on June 3, 2013

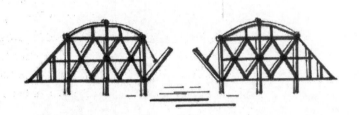

Skydiving at Seventy-Three

Don't ever give up on life!

When a heavy cloak of depression settles down upon my shoulders, I tend to feel as if life has passed me by. I start to ask myself what the point could possibly be, and when I'm unable to answer that question I give up hope, and start resigning myself to my fate. Why even try? When I'm in that awful mind-space I genuinely believe that nothing good or new or exciting will ever happen to me again. Ever. And I'll spend the rest of my life alone. Forever.

And then I proceed to catch up on my sleep.

What usually snaps me out of this mindset is either planning something that I can look forward to, or a heaping helping of reality. That reality usually takes on the form of an event that shows me how erroneous my thought process is. In other words, I get embarrassed out of my depression.

First of all, relatively speaking, my life is pretty darned good. It takes but a minute to read stories of how nasty, brutish and short the average human life can be. For example, how can I possibly feel sorry for myself after looking at photos of the Syrian refugee camps?

But the greatest balm is when I'm inspired by someone who hasn't given up. In this instance it was all the more stunning because it came in the form of a friend. I love being in awe of friends.

From deep beneath my heavy cloak of gloom I happened to peek out at Facebook the other day and saw that my friend Carole, on the brink of her 73rd birthday, had posted footage of herself jumping out of an airplane. A perfectly good airplane. On purpose. Whoa.

You may not be able to control how people feel about you, but you can do unexpected and exciting things at any age. You can skydive. The sky isn't the limit. The sky is the starting point. You can be amazing. And that sounds a lot more appealing to me than lying in bed with the sheets pulled up over my head.

Thanks, Carole.

First published on <u>*September 27, 2015*</u>

Some of Us Don't

It's actually okay not to be great at everything you try.

After taking a semester of one-on-one guitar lessons many years ago, my instructor decided to be brutally honest with me. He said, "Barb, some of us have it, and some of us don't. And you don't."

When I tell that story, a lot of people are outraged at that teacher, but actually I appreciated his comment. Deep down, I knew it was true. I am no guitar player. I would much rather that someone tell me the truth, rather than waste my time and my money and fill me with false hope.

The brutal reality is that we can't all be good at everything we try to do. Trust me when I tell you that you don't want me to sing, either. Or weld. Or skateboard.

We live in a society that tries to tell us that we can do anything that we set our minds to, but that's unrealistic. Yes, some things we can all learn. Facts and figures. Those things just take effort. But others, the things that take a certain level of talent or skill, you will either do well or you won't. Eventually you'll figure out where you stand. It may take time. Some things take years to learn. By all means give things a try if they are important to you.

But there's usually a point, and deep down you know it, when it's time to focus elsewhere if you haven't risen to a level that you are content with in a given field. You don't have to be the best, by the way. But you do have to be satisfied with your level of proficiency.

I'm perfectly okay with the fact that I can't play the guitar. I mean, it would have been cool to be able to do so, but I am quite good at other things. I would like to think that writing is one of them.

If we were all uniformly good at everything, this would be a monochrome world. There would be no challenges. There would be no reason to go to concerts or art galleries or sporting events.

Nothing would be special or outstanding or amazing.

I like being in awe of people. And I like being proud of myself. I like knowing that there are things I do better than others, but for that to work for everyone then there has to be, purely from a mathematical standpoint, things that I do worse than others. If that means I won't be playing Greensleeves on a Gibson any time soon, that's a sacrifice I'm willing to make.

First published on May 23, 2015

Spring!!!

A change of season is one of the most delightful changes of all!

Today is the first day of spring, and I couldn't be more excited. You have to understand, I haven't seen spring in 40 years. In Florida we had two seasons: Summer and January. So this is a huge deal for me.

Even the thought of breaking out a different set of clothes has me grinning like an idiot. And I love that things (including me) actually *look* different from one season to the next here. Maybe you take that for granted, but I gaze upon the blooming flowers where a few weeks ago there were none, and I see it as the natural miracle that it is.

I even ran out and bought a bunch of flowering plants and planted them in the yard of my rental house. And I hate yard work. I'm not sure my landlord will be thrilled that I'm digging holes in the yard, so mum's the word. (Pardon the pun.)

And I made it through a winter! I had my doubts. (Especially when the heater died in my car.) The ever-shortening days felt ominous and unnatural to me.

But we've come out the other side! Joy! Life! Renewal! A visible marker of the passage of time! Is this what spring fever feels like? I'd forgotten. I feel like taking off my clothes and rolling naked amongst the tulips. And that's a problem, because there's a tulip festival in my near future...

First published on <u>*March 20, 2015*</u>

Barb Abelhauser

Thank Your Hands

*Take some time to appreciate
the hard work your hands do for you.*

Nine months ago, I fell down a flight of stairs, dislocated my thumb, stupidly popped it back into place on my own with a resounding crunch (I sometimes have a freakishly high threshold of pain), and the result was a nasty case of De Quervain's Tendonitis in my dominant hand.

I was in agony and a wrist brace for a long, long time. I could barely write. I couldn't lift things. I couldn't shake hands. Even wiping my own behind became a challenge. I only slept sporadically due to the pain. I shed more than a few tears of frustration.

Recently, though, after several unsuccessful non-invasive attempts to resolve the problem, I finally resorted to surgery. That was a little scary because they had to cut the sheath tendon, which is a bracelet type tendon that keeps all the tendons that radiate down from your hand to your forearm in place. And to cut it, they had to move a nerve bundle, which meant if things went wrong I wouldn't have feeling in my hand anymore. That's a rather daunting proposition.

After the surgery I had a hard cast on my wrist and hand for a week. Cooking was difficult. Showering one-handed was not fun. And if I thought I had trouble wiping my butt before...

The good news is that the surgery was a success, and while I'm still healing, most of the time I feel pretty much back to normal. It only took nine months. I will never take my hands for granted again.

You shouldn't, either. You have no idea how much you use your hands in the course of a day until you can't anymore. Your hands are the most unsung heroes in your life. They really deserve some appreciation. Maybe some nice lotion or a hand massage.

Trust me, it's the very least you can do.

First published on <u>September 9, 2015</u>

Thank You, More Please

It never hurts to acknowledge the abundance in the universe.

I was killing time over the weekend on the deadliest of time-killers: Youtube. I came across a light romantic comedy called "*Happythankyoumoreplease*". The title alone got me curious. Plus, Josh Radnor is in it, and he's pure sweet candy to my eyes, so why not?

It's a cute movie. It doesn't surprise me that it didn't win any Oscars. It's not that kind of vehicle. But it was a pleasant way to spend an hour and a half.

One of the things I love most about life is that you never know where or when you're going to be pelted with a pearl of wisdom. In one scene, Malin Akerman, the actress who plays Annie, was telling a story about a time she was in this cab and the driver told her that she had a lot to give, but her problem was that she didn't express enough appreciation. When she asked him how she should do that, he told her to simply say thank you, and always add "more, please," because with gratitude the universe is eternally abundant.

When I heard that, I almost felt a mental click. It just makes so much sense to me. Even if you don't believe in the laws of attraction, or a higher power or anything even remotely new age or spiritual or crunchy-granola, it just seems right to remind yourself that not only should you feel grateful, but that you deserve good things.

I have always liked to take a moment and look up at the sky and thank the universe, even for simple things like the feeling of wind on my face. Now, I plan to add "more, please" to that thank you. At the very least it will influence my attitude. That's a bigger payoff than the average lottery ticket, right?

First published on January 19, 2016

That Certain Something

Six-packs aren't what make me smile.

The older I get, the less I care about the physical attributes of a potential partner. Anyone who is obsessed with washboard stomachs and full heads of hair when they're pushing 50 is not being realistic. Certainly, be well groomed and have a grasp of personal hygiene, but I'm not expecting a hard body.

What attract me most are those qualities that you can't always detect at first glance. Intelligence peppered with a sense of humor. Curiosity. A generous nature. Compassion. Kindness. Decency. A willingness to make a fool of oneself for loved ones. Integrity. Not taking oneself too seriously. A willingness to kill spiders if you hear me scream.

Am I asking too much? I don't think so. *I* have all those qualities. Maybe what I'm looking for is me. But seriously, I see glimmers of that person everywhere. In the man who clearly adores his disabled child and would do anything to make her smile. In the guy who volunteers to help build a house for Habitat for Humanity. In the professor who gives that riveting yet entertaining TED talk.

It's the way you live your life that will move people. Just be yourself and pursue your passions. Embrace your life. It will show. There's no more powerful pheromone on earth than that.

First published on June 28, 2014

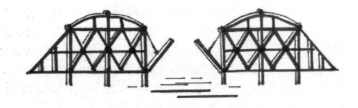

The Cheerleaders in Your Life

Three cheers for emotional support!!!

Starting at around 7th grade, I developed a potent and bitter dislike of cheerleaders that lasted right on through my time at university.

I would never have admitted this then, but I was jealous. They were all beautiful and thin and popular and coordinated and never seemed to get pimples, and knew how to wear makeup and had the confidence to rock a miniskirt. Those were all qualities that seemed very out of reach to me. (Actually, they still feel pretty out of reach, if I'm honest.)

Over time I've learned that there are other fantastic qualities to have, such as intelligence and compassion and integrity, and those will stand the test of time long after your miniskirt days are over. I really like who I am. I'm finding that these traits may not be visible at first glance, and therefore I still struggle to get dates, but I'd *totally* date me.

Another thing that's changed over time is my view of cheerleaders. Now I don't disdain them. I cultivate them. Not the sporting kind. The kind that encourage you. The kind that sing your praises. The kind that say, "You go, girl!!!" Everybody needs that kind of positivity in their lives.

Because of this, I also try to be a cheerleader. I go out of my way to give sincere compliments. I want to be uplifting. In this world there will be plenty of people who will try to drag you down. Do your best to surround yourself with those who will cheer for you, and make an effort to cheer for them as well. Maybe your pom poms aren't as perky as the next person's, but your words will still give them spirit.

Rah rah!

First published on January 9, 2016

The Fine Art of Begging

It's an amazing gift to learn who your friends really are.

Recently I racked up $9,000.00 in debt by moving 3100 miles across country to start my life over after a series of setbacks that, frankly, are becoming too boring to even discuss. Everybody has problems, right? But a friend suggested I do a crowdfunding campaign through the Indiegogo website to help me get my head above water. I set a goal of 5k for my two month campaign, never really expecting to get a response.

The campaign ended just the other day, and much to my shock and awe I did reach 50 percent of my goal. But even more valuable than the money was all that I learned from the experience, about myself and about others. I never realized what a ride it would be until I hopped on.

First of all, as one might expect, it's kind of humiliating to have to beg for money. Essentially, you are telling the entire world, "I can't do this on my own." No one likes to admit that.

Second, you spend a great deal of time dealing with the complex issue that a certain percentage of people are bound to assume that you are asking for something that you don't really deserve because you're lazy or you're a scammer. There's really no simple way to protest your innocence. "I am not a crook" didn't work for Nixon, and it wouldn't have worked for me, either.

And then, at least for me, there was a nagging feeling that maybe it was true. Maybe I didn't really deserve help. I can think of at least a billion people who are worse off than I will ever be. Who do I think I am? What makes me so special? Those are really uncomfortable questions to have to wrestle with.

The moment the campaign was launched, the vultures started circling. "For just $200.00, I can make your campaign go viral!" "Sign up for tips on how to increase your visibility." These emails made me really uncomfortable. It was like my financial desperation had somehow become a business opportunity. For me, this wasn't business. This was my life.

Also, I got some really weird reactions from distant family members. One even told me that what I was doing was inappropriate and an embarrassment to the family. Wow. Several of them still aren't speaking to me, and the irony is, none of them helped out, even emotionally, and I never expected that they would. They had never stepped up before, so it would have surprised me if they did now.

But the amazing thing, the thing that still brings tears of gratitude to my eyes, are the people who did step up. Many of them, I know for a fact, are struggling themselves, and they were often the most generous. Then there were the people from my distant past, many of whom I hadn't had contact with in decades, who supported me without hesitation. And total strangers who said, "I've been where you are. Here. Good luck." Some people said, "I wish I could contribute, but I have no money to give. But I wanted you to know that I heard your story and I'm pulling for you." Even those who just shared a link to my campaign on their Facebook pages hold a special place in my heart.

I am humbled by everyone who supported me emotionally as well as financially. The memories of that will be more precious than gold long after this debt is nothing but a bad memory. And some day when I'm able, I plan to pay this generosity forward. That's a promise.

It is when you have to bare your soul and humble yourself way beyond your comfort zone that you truly discover who your friends are, and that the world is a generous place, indeed. What a gift.

First published on <u>*October 16, 2014*</u>

The Gift of Deprivation

I could sum this up in three words: Less is more.

Oh joy! The sun is out! The sky is blue! I feel like dancing. At this time of year in Seattle, sunshine is a precious gift; one not to be taken for granted. It's like manna from heaven. You can almost hear a choir singing down every solar ray. Laaaaaaa...

On the other hand, in Florida I dreaded the sun. It was always there, sucking the life out of me, making the air as thick and humid as bathwater, covering me in sticky, stinky sweat. I used to scoff at the tourists who reveled in it until they burned to a crisp.

Having had sun poisoning before, I can tell you that it is a most unpleasant experience. I literally turned purple. I blistered. I had a fever and vomited for days. I longed for a peaceful death. After that it became normal for me to avoid the sun at all costs.

But here in Seattle when the sun comes out, you cherish it. You revel in it. You rejoice!

It seems like a contradiction, but by being deprived of the sun, I have been given the gift of the sun! I shall never take it for granted again. How lucky am I? Deprivation is the best thing that has ever happened to me.

First published on February 27, 2016

The Gift of Friendship

Friends are what make you truly rich.

I watched my laptop hit the floor and I heard it break. I stood there for a minute, not wanting to actually open it up and look, wanting to hold on to a few more seconds of being a person who had a computer, and knowing I was about to become a person who didn't have one.

Upon closer inspection, I discovered that I had actually bent the battery. I didn't even know that was possible. And the screen was shattered and partially separated from the keyboard. It was a lost cause. So that was it, then. I was done. No money to replace the laptop, which meant no more blog, no more extra income, nothing to keep me sane during the long, lonely graveyard shifts on the bridge.

Oh, how I cried. And I felt kind of stupid being so devastated over an inanimate object, especially when I'm ever more conscious of the pervading, insidious societal urge toward crass consumerism, but I have come to rely on my laptop, and I honestly and truly had no idea what to do.

Then my friend Ray stepped up and loaned me one of his old ones. What a relief. While it didn't solve the problem, it took the pressure off until I could figure out what to do. And it kept me connected and working and writing. Ray kept me going, as he so often does. I'll always be grateful for that.

So I trundled on like that for a while, but I knew I couldn't use his laptop forever. Not that he was putting any pressure on me at all. Quite the contrary. It's just that I needed to have my own computer. If I was going to risk dropping something on the floor and destroying it, it should be something I own. But I was still at a loss. It's not like a big sweaty wad of cash was going to drop out of the sky.

And then a miracle happened in the form of my friend Martin. Martin, who I've known for seven years, but only in the virtual world of Second Life. I was lamenting my situation to him, and he offered to buy me a laptop. Just like that. He said, "I can afford to help you, and I want to."

That generous.
That kind.
That rare.

My instinct was to turn his offer down. It was too much. But he wanted to give me this gift. He wanted to, and I needed help.

So here I am, writing this on my brand new laptop! A laptop given to me by a true friend.

The thing itself is not what's valuable, even though it's fantastic and a complete life saver. No. It's the love behind it, the decency, the unselfishness, the spirit of giving.

Every day when I use this laptop, I will think of Martin and what he did for me, and I'll remember that there really are people in this world who are willing to go the extra mile, the extra thousand miles actually, for a friend.

I hope someday, when my head is actually above water financially, I can pass on the bounty to someone else in their time of need. In the meantime, though, I will do my best to be there for friends in other ways, such as being a good listener and a source of support, and I can delight in the fact that with friends such as these, I'm rich in the only way that truly matters.

So I'll leave you with this quote from the movie It's a Wonderful Life: "No man is a failure who has friends."

Thank you for being one of those, dear reader.

First published on <u>*December 25, 2013*</u>

The Little Things

The most unexpected things can bring you pure joy.

On my drive to work today I got tears in my eyes; tears of gratitude. I came around a curve and saw a tree with flaming red leaves.

You don't see too many trees whose leaves change in the fall in this Emerald City of Seattle, but you see enough. Enough to make you appreciate them even more.

I am back in a place where leaves change color! I can't explain how much that means to someone who hasn't seen it in 30 years.

There are so many other things here that bring me back to the climate of my childhood.

Moss. Rocks. The smell of rich, dark earth. Soft grass. Water that actually tastes good. It's all so precious to me.

Priceless, because it took so much for me to get to this place of abundance. So forgive me for being maudlin, but tears are bound to flow.

Abundance is mine!

First published on <u>October 20, 2014</u>

Perfect Moments

Some experiences are so perfect that you can never forget them.

Andy Warhol said that we'd all get 15 minutes of fame. To that I say, "Pffft, what's the point?" If you're the type that wants fame, having only 15 minutes of it would be cruel at best. Fortunately, fame is not nearly as important to me as experiencing perfect moments in time.

Have you ever experienced one of those fleeting instants in your life when everything seems to come together and you know you'll hold that memory close at hand for as long as you live? I honestly believe that those are the moments you will see when your life flashes before your eyes. Those brief interludes are when you get to taste pure joy. I have had a few. They always sneak up on me.

One time I was sitting on a lawn chair on a beach in Puerto Rico. The temperature was perfect, and there was a slight breeze. I had no place that I had to be. The surf was rolling onto the shore, and there seemed to be a million stars in the sky. I saw the Southern Cross just above the horizon. And BAM.

There I was. In a perfect moment.

Another time I was standing on a rooftop in Istanbul, and all of a sudden all the mosques in the area began the call to prayer as I gazed over the city. It had taken quite a bit to get myself to that city, and yet there I was. Again, a perfect moment.

And then there's every single solitary time I look at the full moon.

Then there was the time I stepped out my front door and the entire sky was, I swear to God, bright yellow. I have no idea why. And I've never seen anything like that before or since. But it was like I was on another planet. Everyone in the park across the street was just standing there, staring skyward. I wanted to take a picture, but that would have meant going inside to find my camera, and I didn't want to miss a single second of it.

Another time I was swimming in a crystal clear cove in Dubrovnik, Croatia. I have never seen water so pure or a day so fine. Heaven could not be better.

The first perfect moment I remember was as a child in Connecticut. I was sitting on a rocking chair in the living room with all the lights out except those on the Christmas tree. I was in my pajamas and wrapped in a soft blanket. Safe and warm. And I just happened to look over my shoulder just as it started to snow for the first time that winter. Bliss.

The moment I cherish most, perhaps, is the first time I stood at the Craggy Gardens overlook on the Blue Ridge Parkway and I knew, I mean, I KNEW this was where I was supposed to be. This was what home felt like. I could breathe. I've been trying to get back there ever since.

Who needs fame? If I get 15 perfect moments in time, I'll consider myself fortunate indeed.

First published on June 24, 2013

Barb Abelhauser

The Stupidity of Loneliness

Note to self: Memorize this and recite it at least once a month.

I had an epiphany the other day. Loneliness really makes no sense at all. It's the mistaken assumption that someone out there, whom you've yet to even meet, holds the key to your happiness. How absurd.

First of all, from a mathematical standpoint that would also mean that I hold the key to some stranger's happiness, and I'm keyless and clueless. So that formula is easily disproven. (And I don't even like math.)

Also, loneliness means you're giving all your power away. I don't like that concept at all. I'm not going to live in some emotional limbo, on the off chance that some random person is going to come along and care enough and be capable enough to fill my every emotional need.

Ever since I had this epiphany about two weeks ago, I haven't felt lonely at all.

It's like a weight has lifted off my shoulders. I sort of feel as though I'm back in the driver's seat of my life. What a liberating feeling.

Not that I plan to go live in a cave in the wilderness, mind you. I still want friends. I still want companionship. I still have itches that I very much would like to have scratched. But suddenly the urgency is no longer there. The sadness is gone. I appreciate my life for what it is, and look forward to what it can be, in whatever form that may take.

I hope this feeling lasts.

First published on August 3, 2015

The Voices in My Head

I just thought of something else my beloved late boyfriend used to say. "Even if you pour syrup all over something, that doesn't make it a pancake." Oh, how I miss him.

First of all, don't panic. They're good voices. Well... mostly.

I still hear my late boyfriend all the time. For example, if I said I really, really liked something, he'd turn that into the best compliment ever. I might say, "This is really good tomato soup," and he'd reply, "You're my tomato soup of love." So now whenever I like something, he's with me.

I also often hear my mother holding forth with life lessons, such as, "Life isn't fair," even though she passed away 25 years ago. These pearls of wisdom can sometimes be irritating, but hey, she meant well. And she was often right.

I can still hear the humorous and pithy commentary of a friend I had for 14 years, even though he no longer speaks to me for reasons that I will never understand.

And I'll quite often replay delightful conversations I've had with people. That explains the vague smile I have on my face when I appear to be daydreaming. It sure beats having "It's a Small World after All" stuck in my head. (Gotcha!)

And we can all predict what someone might say in a given situation if we know that person really well. The operative word there is "might". Don't get into the habit of then attributing that stuff to the person as if they've actually said it. I used to know someone who would get pissed off at people based on imaginary conversations. That does not serve you well, and it can be quite confusing to those around you.

Unfortunately, most of us can hear hurtful things that have been said to us in the past as if that thing is being said, clear as day, right this minute. That's why it's so important to choose your words carefully. It's amazing how long your voice can echo without you even realizing it.

But I have to say that for the most part, I really, really like the voices in my head.

"You're the voices in my head... of love..."

Thanks, Chuck. I know. And I'm grateful for that gift.

First published on June 10, 2016

The World's Best Bedside Manner

Some people just have a natural gift of making you feel at ease.

Recently I had surgery on my wrist. I was scared silly. Mostly because I'd be all alone during my recovery, but also because it's downright unnatural to voluntarily subject oneself to getting sliced open. I mean, seriously, who in their right mind says, "Here. Cut me, please." You have to be in a heck of a lot of pain in order to seek out pain as a remedy for that pain. After many months of procrastinating, I had reached that point.

I had every confidence in my surgeon. Her name is Dr. Elizabeth Joneschild, and she's part of the Seattle Hand Surgery Group. I'd seen her several times prior to this last, surgical resort, so I had developed a great professional relationship with her. Not only does she clearly know what she's doing, but she's very patient when you ask her questions, has an excellent reputation, and, let's face it, she wouldn't have an office with such a spectacular view if she weren't doing something right. So if you have problems with your hand or wrist, I highly recommend her.

The anesthesiologist, on the other hand, I only got to meet on the morning of the surgery. That's, of course, pretty standard, but it doesn't do much to inspire confidence. Here's someone who can knock you out in a variety of ways, who you don't meet until he's about to knock you out.

In this case, I was to remain conscious. They were only numbing the arm and putting a drape across so I couldn't see what was happening (for which I was extremely grateful). But I was still scared and I've no doubt that it showed.

But I was lucky enough to have Dr. Stephen Markowitz as my anesthesiologist. I've known a lot of great people in the medical field in my lifetime, but this guy really went the extra mile. Obviously Dr. J had to concentrate on what she was doing, so Dr. M started asking me about my job. What's it like to be a bridgetender? What bridge do you work on? How high is it above the water? Any question he could think of.

Not only did this conversation distract me, but (and I have no idea if he was conscious that he was doing this or not) it also allowed my mind to leave a realm where I was feeling pretty helpless and scared, and enter a realm where I was an expert and actually had something to teach and contribute. The surgery was over in about 15 minutes, and I didn't feel a thing, not even panic. What a gift.

I've got to say that my hand was definitely in good hands. I'll be forever grateful for that. When you only have two of something, you tend to want to hold on to them at all costs.

First published on July 25, 2015

Thirty Yards Deep

Achievements are all the more spectacular for being hard-won.

My childhood was full of dysfunction and poverty and abuse. A lot more people can say that than we as a society would care to admit. Beneath this civilized façade is a nasty and brutish reality for many of us, and that shapes who we are.

When you grow up in a really screwed up environment, it effects your ability to trust, to feel safe, to be confident. It twists your concept of what you deserve. It colors the way you view the world.

I say all this to explain, not to excuse, who I am. I don't think my past gives me a free pass. I just think it means I probably have to work a bit harder to get where I'm going. But I can still get there, and those achievements will be all the sweeter for having been hard-won.

I'm not into sports, but someone said something to me the other day that really struck a chord in me. She said:

"Given the fact that you started out 30 yards deep in your own end zone, it's really impressive that you want to play the game at all, let alone have scored so many touchdowns."

Yup. I think I'm willing to own that.

First published on January 2, 2015

Those Popcorn Moments

*Don't overlook the most basic things
that bring you joy from day to day.*

I was talking to a friend the other day and she said that as a single mother money was always tight, so she didn't get to travel. Even though she didn't really consider it a major regret, that kind of made me feel guilty because I've been to 22 countries.

It's been a while since I was able to afford to even buy a plane ticket, but I want to get back to that point eventually. I live in hope.

I never had kids. I've never even had cable TV or a smart phone, so it's all about priorities. If you want something badly enough, you'll make sacrifices and you'll work toward it. You may or may not be successful in reaching your goals, but you'll make the effort.

Child rearing was not an effort I was willing to make, but I admire anyone who happily takes on that responsibility.

Another friend said she didn't regret not being able to travel because she got just as much pleasure from sitting on the couch with her daughter, eating a bowl of popcorn and watching a movie. I think that's a wonderful attitude. You should make the most of what you have, and have a clear sense of what makes you happy.

Make plans, sure, but make your popcorn wherever you happen to be sitting in life. Don't wait. Because when all is said and done, you shouldn't deprive yourself of those popcorn moments. They count for a lot.

First published on <u>April 21, 2016</u>

Thoughts on Gratitude

*Work toward your goals, but appreciate
the here and now as well.*

I've been thinking about gratitude quite a bit lately. In fact, it's
going to be the subject of my first anthology. As a topic it's
much more complex and richly nuanced than I first thought.
I'm finding that the more I view my life in terms of gratitude,
the more blessings I seem to receive. There's something about
the mere act of sincerely acknowledging the abundance in your
life, putting it out there in the universe that you realize that
these things are gifts, not privileges. This seems to attract even
more abundance.

The more pragmatic side of me thinks that it's not actually that
you're getting more positivity. It's more that you're becoming
attuned to the largesse that was always there. Perhaps you
have just taken it for granted, or have been focused on the
more negative aspects of your life.

Crunchy granola gifts or clear-eyed perspective? Either way, I'll
take it! Thank you. More, please.

While discussing this with friends, I was asked, "Can gratitude
ever be inappropriate?" That question intrigued me quite a bit.
I suspect that gratitude in general is very influenced by the
culture in which you find yourself. People in some countries
just seem to be much more instinctively gracious than those in
others.

Is one viewpoint better than another? The fact that we have coined terms such as "obsequious", with its seemingly negative connotations, would lead one to believe that there is such a thing as too much gratitude.

I tend to think that any gratitude, if sincere and genuine, is not misplaced. But who am I to judge? I'm just happy to be here!

First published on <u>*June 2, 2016*</u>

Time Capsules

One way or another, we all make an impact.

Just before I moved to Seattle, I drove over to the house I used to own in Florida to say goodbye to it. I almost drove past it without recognizing it, such were the number of improvements the current owner had made. That was kind of disconcerting.

One of the things that he changed was the front steps, which I had toiled over to make unique looking, and yet safer for my elderly neighbors. I remember drawing a crowd as I used my sledge hammer and framed my bricks. I was really proud of myself.

When the current owner undid my hard work, I wonder if he found my time capsule. I left pictures and mementos and wrote about what my life was like living in that house. I assumed that capsule would be there for more than the twenty years it lasted.

Time capsules have always intrigued me. They're little messages that you send into the future. They allow you to feel as though you own a little piece of immortality.

In a way, that's one of the reasons people have children. It's how you continue the life of your family far beyond your own life. I often wonder about my distant ancestors. Could they have possibly conceived of the life I'm living now, thanks to them? Did they even have time to give me that much thought? They are strangers to me, and their lives, for the most part, were nasty, brutish and short. Did they ever get the chance to gaze up at the stars and think about the future?

If you're like me, you'd like to have a lasting impact upon the world. You'd like to make a positive difference. Without even realizing it consciously, most of us are sending out quiet little time capsules. We write, we create, we give advice, we start traditions and family stories and build things. We inspire. We make history.

And quite often, the beneficiaries of these time capsules will never know who sent them. Who started the movement that changed that law? Who was the first one to touch the toe of that statue for good luck? Where did my blue eyes come from?

Just by virtue of being alive, we all stand upon the time capsules, both literal and figurative, of the past, and send time capsules into the future as well.

First published on January 18, 2016

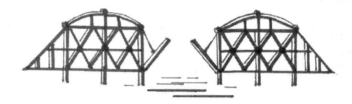

Traditions

If you don't have any, make some up!
Traditions are what connect you to the wider world.

Despite the overwhelming weight of traditions as described in <u>Fiddler on the Roof</u>, I've always admired people who have them. Whether they be national or religious or cultural or simply family traditions, these customs help to bind each of us to a greater whole.

Coming from a fairly nomadic and rootless family, I don't have very many of these habits to fall back on. But we do have a few. For example, we always shake the milk before pouring it. This came about because my grandfather was a dairy farmer. If you get raw milk directly from the cow, the cream tends to separate if you don't shake it back up. So we shake the milk to this day even though it no longer needs it.

When we go to the movies, we always whisper "Previews are my favorite part" at the very beginning. I don't know why, and it isn't even always true, but we do it nonetheless.

And when traveling long distances by car, when we get close to our destination we say, "Smell the salt?" That's because when my mother was a child they'd take family trips to Long Island, and they knew they were almost there when they started smelling the salt water.

And I've invented a few traditions of my own. Each year I'll buy a Christmas ornament that reminds me of something from the past year. And I always make red, white and blue fruit salad (strawberries, green grapes, and blueberries) to eat while watching the Independence Day fireworks. And one I particularly like is the one where I blow all my worries and concerns over my shoulder whenever I cross a state line when I travel. Leave that stuff behind. Don't take it on your trip. Like it or not, you can always pick it back up when you get home.

Customs. Habits, Rituals. Beliefs. They're what connect us and define us. If you don't have them, then make the effort to create your own and define yourself.

First published on April 23, 2013

Unplug

Sometimes you just have to take a breath.

Recently a friend of mine posted some quotations by the author Anne Lamott on her Facebook page. One that really struck a chord with me was this one:

"Almost everything will work again if you unplug it for a few minutes, including you."

Wise words indeed. I thought of them last night when my wifi went dead at a critical moment. I was really feeling frustrated as I unplugged the modem and slowly counted off a minute. And I decided that rather than stand there gritting my teeth as the seconds clicked slowly by, I'd do some stretching exercises based on a vague memory of the last yoga class I attended.

Why did I stop doing yoga? I have never felt physically better than when I did it regularly. I have no idea. Time. Money. Habit. Pure laziness. I need to get back into it. I need to give myself that gift.

I also thought about how wonderful my recent day trip to the tulip festival was. I could feel my blood pressure drop. I could feel myself relax and breathe. These things are important.

I need to be more gentle with myself. Take more baths. Take more breaks. Take more naps. Soak up the sun.

I need to be kinder to myself. I need to remember that no one can be as kind to me as I can be to myself. Deep down I know what I need. I also know that while it is necessary to do those things that will allow me to live my life (Damned job! Damned housework!) it is also vital that I not forget to do those things that make life worthwhile.

Then I did one last luxurious stretch, plugged my modem back in, and sure enough, both my laptop and I were good to go again.

First published on April 15, 2015

Untapped Beauty

Amazing to come across something beautiful
that you've never seen before.

God, but I love the internet. It introduces me to things I didn't previously know existed on an almost daily basis. There is so much in this world that can shock or amaze or awe.

Just the other day I happened to go to the Bing website and was presented with a gorgeous picture of a Chinese Lantern Fruit. Whoa. What *is* that?

I'd never seen anything like it in my life. I naturally had to learn more about it. It turns out it's more formally known as *Physalis Alkekengi*.

When the fruit first forms, it's covered by a delicate-looking papery husk that resembles a Chinese lantern.

Hence the name. Over time, the husk dries out and becomes more filigreed, exposing the fruit to view.

Isn't nature awesome? Such delicacy, such artistry. Such intense beauty. It leaves me speechless.

Upon further research though, I've decided I will never sample this fascinating fruit, because according to a Wikipedia article, it's used as a diuretic, antiseptic, liver corrective and sedative.

But I guess my whole reason for babbling on about this beautiful creation is that is makes me wonder what else is out there that is equally stunning that I've yet to discover.
I get excited just thinking about the possibilities.

I don't think there's any better feeling in this world than that of being certain of future awe. (I need to invent a word for that.) It almost makes you look forward to the sound of your alarm clock, doesn't it?

First published on <u>March 12, 2015</u>

Untapped Depths

I wish I had the time and ability to hear everyone's story.
We all have them.

Every day we walk or drive past countless numbers of people without communicating with them in any meaningful way. That's perfectly natural. It would be impossible to gct anything done if we stopped to have intense conversations with everyone we encountered.

But lately I have been viewing all these strangers with fresh eyes. That's because I've participated in a few storytelling events by a meet up group here in Seattle called <u>Fresh Ground Stories</u>. The stories that are told at this event have to be true and personal, and boy, are they ever.

We all look at people without speaking to them and tend to make certain assumptions, but this group demonstrates loudly and clearly that there is much more to people than meets the eye. Whether it's the petite young girl who had been abused by her father all her life and then finally confronted him as an adult, or the guy who made a documentary about a quirky homeless man, or the transgender woman who had struggled to feel accepted all her life, or the man who lost 100 pounds and overcame social anxiety, every person has a story, and often it's a fascinating one.

Now when I see strangers on the street, I kind of have regrets. I may be passing over someone who has an amazing history that would enrich my life in its very telling. That guy might have been in the crowd when President Kennedy was assassinated. That lady might be the daughter of a suffragette. I'll never know.

As I go about my daily business these days, people seem to have more density, more substance to them. I often think, "What's your story?" I wish I had time to hear them all.

First published on <u>July 19, 2015</u>

Walk Your Life

Life lessons can come from the most unexpected places.

I've been watching a BBC series called Tribal Wives on Youtube lately. The premise is that they have a British woman live with a remote tribe for a month and take on the role of a Tribal Wife. Women have been sent to Thailand, Gabon, Mexico, and Namibia, to name a few locations.

It's really fascinating to watch someone cope after being forced to cast off all the modern "comforts" of life, such as cell phones and indoor plumbing. It's interesting to see them struggle with the day in and day out grueling work that comes with living rough. For many women in the world, life is really, really hard.

But what I enjoy most is seeing what inevitably happens. These women generally assume that they will have nothing to learn from these uneducated, poverty-stricken, deprived people. But by the end of their stay, they discover that there's a certain wisdom that comes from not being distracted by all the extras of modern living. There's a certain glory to just living; just getting on with it.

In the episode I watched today, a woman from London was placed with the Raramuri tribe of Northwest Mexico. This is a woman who spends a lot of her time worrying and overthinking things, and not trusting people. She lives with this tribe, learns their customs and traditions, and works side by side with the women. Her nervous nature becomes all too evident by comparison.

Their advice to her is not to think so much. Basically, she needs to get over it. Just relax and do what needs to be done. The Raramuri have a saying, "Walk your life." Sometimes the most profound insights come in deceptively simple packages.

Just walk your life.

First published on January 29, 2015

Wax On, Wax Off

Routine does not have to equal tedium.

When I work on the new South Park Drawbridge here in
Seattle, one of my duties is to wash the tower windows inside
and out once a month. Given that the building looks similar to
an air traffic control tower and has large windows all around
its perimeter, this not a trifling endeavor. But needless to say,
bridge operators need to be able to see what they're doing, so
it's got to be done.

I did it today and got into a sort of Zen state. I kept thinking of
Mr. Miyagi in the Karate Kid saying, "Wax on, wax off."

Patience.
Calm.
Focus.
Control.
Don't forget to breathe.

Not that what I was doing was difficult. But the best way to
turn routine into tedium is to have a piss poor attitude about it,
and I'd kind of like to avoid that. So I concentrated on being the
best window washer on the face of the earth, if only for that
particular moment in time. My goal became to make the
windows so clear that they became invisible. When the
weather is nice you can see Mount Rainier from here, and I
want people to see every rock and crevice of that beautiful
mountain thanks to me.

When you strive for excellence and really tune in, routines are less of a chore and more of a comfort. My life has been anything but routine of late, so I'm happy to have any sort of habitual task, and look forward to building up more of them over time.

I'm grateful to have this job. I'm excited about the life it will afford me. I love that it allows me to live in this wondrous place. Because of that, I'd gladly wash these windows every single day of the week if need be.

Bring it on.

First published on January 3, 2015

What I Did for Like

Friends. They're worth the effort.

On this particular day of the week I usually don't rise until noon because I don't go to work until 3 pm. So when the alarm went off at 7 am, I experienced some less than charitable thoughts. Especially since my dog Devo had been snoring most of the night. When he does that he sounds like a little old man muttering incomprehensively to himself. It makes me giggle, but it's not conducive to deep sleep.

So I sat up in bed, rubbed my eyes, and thought, "Who does this? Have I completely lost my marbles?" I had agreed to meet a friend for breakfast. Waaaaaaaay on the other side of town. As in 25 miles through downtown Seattle rush-hour traffic. For eggs.

I thought of coming up with a lame excuse and going back to bed. But this is a friend who happens to be an airline pilot (my bff calls him my "flyboy") and he rarely passes through Seattle. When he does it's a high speed chase to catch up with him before he flies out again.

So I stumbled into the shower, then got dressed and hit the road. While sitting in stop and go traffic, I thought back to a time when I wouldn't have considered driving 25 miles for anyone unless there was a good chance of a marriage proposal or at the very least a free car involved. And yet here I was. Stopping and going. What had changed?

It's simple, really. I value true friends much more than I used to. Relocating 3100 miles from home to a place where no one knows you will do that to you. Suddenly friendship, the thing you always had been surrounded by, the thing that defined you, is no longer something you can take for granted.

For me these days, sitting across the table from someone who is genuinely interested in what's going on with my life, and wanting to hear that person's news as well, is a rare and precious opportunity. It's worth more than sleep. It's worth more than gold. It's something to cherish. If I learned nothing else from this massive life change of mine, that lesson made it all worthwhile.

Breakfast with a friend is priceless. I might even have been persuaded to drive more than 25 miles for it. Maybe even 26. And the eggs were all the more delicious for the company.

First published on <u>*April 17, 2015*</u>

What Perishes is Not Real

Perspective. Shared wisdom. Two of life's greatest gifts.

For the life of me, I will never understand people who don't like to read. There is so much wisdom out there. Reading is like accessing the brains of millions of other people. There is more knowledge in this world than one brain could possibly hold. Think of books as thumb drives that enhance the memory of the computer that is you.

For example, a friend of mine reminded me recently of the beginning of one of Rumi's amazing poems.

"Each form you see has its unseen archetype. If the form is transient, its essence is eternal. If you have known beauty in a face or wisdom in a word, let this counsel your heart: what perishes is not real."

"The Body is a Rose" ~ Rumi

Now, I've read Rumi before, and been moved by his words, but I can't keep everything in my head. That's why reading is so important. I particularly needed to hear this passage on the day my friend shared it with me, as I was going through a stressful situation.

Perspective is something I always struggle with. It's hard for me to remember that what I might consider to be a crisis is usually a mere blip on the radar in the overall scheme of things.

So much that I worry about and agonize over is actually trivial when compared with mortality.

I remember being really aware of that right after my boyfriend passed away. People would be griping over how well a coworker was cleaning the toilet, and I'd be thinking, "But you're ALIVE!!! Don't you get it? Who cares about the bloody toilet?"

But with the passage of time, I find myself falling back into my old bad habits of taking things entirely too seriously. So now I try to remember to say "what perishes is not real" as often as possible. Perspective.

First published on <u>*January 16, 2016*</u>

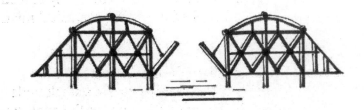

What's Important

Revel in the fact that your source of joy is unique unto you.

I just gave my new dog Quagmire a stuffed squeaky toy, and for about a half hour, his life was complete. He ran around the house squeaking it at random, shaking it within an inch of its life and covering it with slobber. Then he ruthlessly ripped its little head off and coated the bed in stuffing. I don't think he's ever known such joy.

For a brief shining moment, nothing else mattered to Quagmire. I suspect I could have waved a rare steak under his nose and he wouldn't have noticed. He was in the zone. Pure bliss.

If someone were to give me a stuffy, I wouldn't reach such heights of ecstasy. But there are other things that do it for me. (That steak wouldn't hurt.)

It's kind of fascinating that each one of us has a different source of joy. It's also probably the only reason our society can maintain itself. If there were only one thing that made all of us happy, we'd soon be fighting over that thing, and none of us would be able to enjoy it.

So seek out your equivalent of a stuffy, and shake it silly! And don't let anyone make you feel silly for doing so! Do your thing.

The fact that we're each unique is the best possible thing that could have happened to us. It sort of makes you wonder why we are so hell-bent on discriminating against others for their differences. Thank God for the differences, I say! That way I can have my stuffy all to myself!

First published on June 1, 2016

What's That on Your Forehead?

Appreciate your unique talents!

My dog Blue has a white streak on his forehead. It's pretty standard coloring for Italian Greyhounds, but I absolutely love it. When we're cuddling and I run my finger along that streak I often think about the fact that he isn't even aware that it's there, and there is, of course, no way to tell him about it. That prominent feature, as far as he's concerned, doesn't even exist.

Humans are much more self-aware. When we look in the mirror, we know that we're gazing at our own image. And we can, to a certain extent, imagine how others must see us. We can be proud. We can be embarrassed. We are definitely aware of the figurative streaks on our foreheads, for better or for worse.

But we all have other kinds of streaks. Character streaks, spiritual streaks, streaks covered by a thick blanket of denial. Cruel people are either psychopaths or they do not see the impact they have on the people around them. And as they say in the movie "When Harry met Sally", everyone thinks they have good taste and a sense of humor, but we can't all have good taste and a sense of humor.

But when I am sitting there cuddling with Blue, I like to ponder those positive streaks that often go overlooked. Streaks of potential. Streaks of talent. Streaks that we discount. Personal gifts that we all have, and may not even realize are there, despite the fact that everyone else can see them as plain as day.

I didn't really know I had an artistic streak until I was about 40 years old. (Check out my work <u>here</u>.) People who are excellent listeners often assume that everyone has that talent, so they don't realize what a positive impact they make on those they care about. Outgoing people don't fully comprehend that some people find social situations excruciatingly painful. Natural born leaders generally don't set out to develop this quality; it's just there.

You hold great promise. You have amazing abilities. Everyone does. Listen to those around you. They probably have been pointing out that streak on your forehead for a long, long time. It's time you appreciate what you have.

First published on <u>June 12, 2013</u>

When Things Go Wrong

Are things not going according to plan?
Who says your plan is the plan?

When your job requires that you open and close a drawbridge and something happens that causes it to malfunction, that's a bad day. That's a stressful, paperwork-generating, workmen-crawling-all-over-your-territory type of day. I don't like those days. Today was one of those days.

But really, since I didn't do anything to break one of the most expensive pieces of equipment owned by the City of Seattle, I shouldn't let it get to me. Nothing went "wrong". Things were just not going according to my plan. It would be arrogant of me to think that my plan was the way things ought to be. I mean, in the grand scheme of things, who am I? If the universe sees fit to drop a bomb in the middle of my flimsy little itinerary, what gives me the right to complain?

Perhaps when I'm feeling as though things have gone wrong, I should try to look at it slightly differently. It's change. Change happens. I need to focus on better ways to identify and adapt to change, rather than panic or grouse or be bothered by things I cannot control.

When you think about it, being rattled by change is about as silly as shouting at the waves for crashing up on the beach. They're going to wash up no matter how big a tantrum I might choose to throw, so perhaps it's time to stop making an existential fool of myself.

While I am capable of making choices in my life (and believe me, I've made some doozies), I am not the driver of destiny's car. Getting too full of myself and thinking I'm steering this thing is what causes me to feel disappointment, frustration, and irritation. All of those feelings are generated by a sense of how things are "supposed" to turn out, when in fact, I haven't a freakin' clue what will happen next, so harboring a set of expectations is absurd.

So I guess from now on I'll let the workmen fix the bridge and accept the fact that one way or another, the universe will take care of itself. Whether I like it or not.

First published on <u>*February 25, 2015*</u>

Women of Character

There's nothing more valuable in life than a true friend.

Looking back at my mother's life from an adult perspective often renders me speechless. When she was 17 her father died, which plunged her family into poverty. I honestly think she got married just to get out of that overcrowded, depressing little house.

By the time I came along she was in the process of divorcing her abusive, alcoholic husband, as well she should have. But that just "wasn't done" in the 60's. She became a neighborhood pariah, and was left to raise three girls alone in the projects with no support whatsoever, neither financial nor emotional, from her ex-husband or anyone else.

Man, that must have been hard. That must have been scary. I'm not sure I would have been able to handle it. I'm sure she needed a friend.

Fortunately, she found one. And what a friend she was. Ann was quite a character. She was strong. She did not suffer fools gladly. She was fiercely loyal. And she didn't take herself too seriously.

One time Ann was having a particularly bad day. One of the lenses had fallen out of her glasses and broken. And then on her way home, her car horn got stuck. So she was driving down the street, horn blaring. Naturally this drew a lot of attention in the neighborhood. She just laughed and stuck her middle finger through the lens-less glasses at people as she drove by. That was Ann in a nutshell.

Eventually Ann became the mayor of our little town, and she also nursed her son through a tragically fatal case of AIDS back before anyone knew what AIDS was. The woman was tough as nails.

Growing up, I remember hearing my mother laughing with her almost daily over coffee at our kitchen table. That just seemed normal to me. But now I see that it was also probably sanity-preserving for both of them.

Friends. What would we do without them?

First published on May 23, 2016

Working on Holidays

*I wrote this one on a Thanksgiving. Be thankful
for those who work so you don't have to.*

I love that more and more people are refusing to shop on the
holidays in order to pressure companies to not force their staff
to spend those days at work. And I love it when I hear of a
company that chooses to do the right thing and close during
those periods.

I will always support organizations that support their
employees.

But while you are enjoying your turkey today, please don't
forget that it's not just the cashiers of this world who are
forced to work on the holidays. As you read this, I'm most likely
working all by myself on this, my favorite holiday, and feeling
kind of lonely because of it. I'll also be working on Christmas
and New Year's Day, just as I worked on Memorial Day and the
4th of July.

As a bridgetender, it kind of goes with the territory. Heaven
forefend that the shipping lanes are not navigable for any
reason. And I'm not alone.

The ambulance drivers, nurses, policemen, cab drivers, 911
operators, security guards and airport personnel of this world
are right here with me, keeping the gears of society turning.

So when you give thanks today, thank those of us who can't sit at the table with you. And maybe bring us a plate.

A little of everything, but hold the cranberries, please. I hate cranberries.

First published on <u>November 26, 2015</u>

You Need Help

Be willing to receive.

I know a lot of people, mostly men, who don't like to accept help from anyone. I'm not just talking about that annoying habit of refusing to ask for directions. (Men must secretly want to kiss the inventor of the GPS on the lips.) No. I mean any kind of help at any time. Like when you get trapped under a heavy object, as you do, and someone comes along with a block and tackle and offers to hoist said object from your person, free of charge. Those "don't help me" types will say, "No thanks. I've got this under control." Suit yourself.

Come to think of it, that's a fairly good indicator of your level of don't-help-me-ness. If people say "suit yourself" to you a lot, you may have a problem. You may want to...uh...get help, because you are overlooking a very valuable social dynamic. You see, people often *want* to help. It makes them feel good. It strengthens bonds. If your neighbor breaks out his jumper cables when your car has a dead battery, he's not only helping you and taking the opportunity to get to know you better, but he's comforting himself with the idea that if *his* battery ever goes dead, you will be there for him.

Helping is also a way for people to show you that they love you. When you have the flu and your Aunt Betty brings you a pot of homemade chicken soup, don't say "You shouldn't have." That may seem like the polite response but what it sounds like is, "I don't think I deserve it," and that makes Aunt Betty feel not only bad for you and your lack of self-esteem, but also irritated that she went to the trouble to pluck all the feathers off her favorite chicken. No, what you should say is, "Thank you so much! I love you, too."

Accepting help may make you feel vulnerable or weak, but think of it as a gift to both you and the giver. You can't give without getting something back. It's impossible. But you also can't give unless someone's willing to receive.

First published on June 6, 2013

You're Alive!

Life is beautiful. Don't take it for granted.

Recently we lost a cultural icon and a great man by the name of Leonard Nimoy, and millions will mourn his passing. At times like this I'm reminded of something I learned the hardest possible way this year. Life is very precious.

I know several people who seem to exist in a constant state of fury and irritation. These people amaze me. I can't relate to them on any level. I want to say to them, "You're *alive!* Don't you get it? You can do anything. You have choices. What the *hell* do you have to be angry about?"

I think these people walk through life with blinders on. They certainly don't realize they are throwing away the most valuable gift in the universe: their very existence. I look at them and think, "What a waste." There are plenty of people who are no longer with us, who appreciated every exquisite moment of the lives they had, who would gladly take even a day of someone's unappreciated lifespan if only they could be alive again.

When you're in a rage, your vision narrows to a tiny little point. You don't see anything around you. You certainly don't take the time to stop and smell the roses. You're too busy pissing all over them. Why would you want to narrow your field of vision like that? There's so much to see! Life is just so freakin' beautiful, people. I wish everyone realized that.

So next time you are angry because someone has cut you off in traffic, try this instead: take a deep breath. Look around. Then drive home and tell the people that you love that you love them. Because that's what matters. Nothing else does.

First published on <u>March 1, 2015</u>

Zzzzzzzzz

Ah, the pure bliss of a good nap!

There's nothing more luxurious, in my opinion, than a long nap on a rainy Saturday afternoon. I revel in turning off the phone, unhooking my bra, kicking off my shoes, putting on something made of flannel, and allowing the mattress to embrace me like a long lost lover. Pure bliss.

Rain is hypnotic. Ocean waves even more so. Put me in the vicinity of a beach and I'll go down like a bag of wet cement.

I love to snooze so much that I don't even have to wait for the rain, or for a Saturday afternoon. I've taken napping to a whole new level. If it were an Olympic sport, I'd get the gold medal for sure.

I often look back at my childhood and laugh. I cannot believe there was ever a time when I would cry when it was time for bed, but I would. I'd pitch a royal fit. Now I'm more apt to cry if I *can't* sleep.

I think I was a dog in a previous life. I greatly admire the way they can go from hyper-hound mode and then heave a sigh and be completely relaxed in less than a second. And if I could sleep 18 hours a day like they do I would. My dogs encourage this. They love to snuggle with me as I sleep, and are thrilled when I do it, as long as it isn't during their mealtimes. (And believe me when I tell you they have inner clocks of Swiss-like precision. They do not hesitate to politely cough in my ear and tap me on the shoulder when it's time for their kibble, vile creatures that they are.)

As much as I complain about working the graveyard shift, one of the few advantages is that I can pretty much sleep any time during the day and no one gives me any guff about it. I have the perfect excuse. Now if I could just get people to stop mowing their lawns.

This is why I long for my own home-based business. I have no problem working 8, 10, even 12 hours a day. Just not consecutively. I hate being held to a schedule.

And then there's the avoidance factor. Some people drink to escape. Others do drugs. I nap. Not only is it a much less expensive habit, but it's much more socially acceptable.

I'd write more, but I feel a nap coming on.

First published on June 22, 2013

Last Day

*Time to celebrate all the important people in your life
by telling them just how much they mean to you.*

Late last year my favorite person in the whole world had a stroke. Ever since then she's had several seizures, another stroke, and has been in and out of comas. When she did come to, she was completely confused, and, basically, "not there". Although her body lingered on, I was already mourning the loss of her essence. For all intents and purposes I had given up hope for my Aunt Betty.

Even if I had lived next door rather than 3000 miles away, I knew we'd never gossip and joke again, and that devastated me.

Then the other day I was on Facebook and her daughter-in-law contacts me via her I-phone. She says Aunt Betty is walking and talking again! She sends me a photo of her, and she looks great.

The head cold that had been stopping up my sinuses so completely that I wasn't convinced I even had nostrils promptly disappeared, and it hasn't come back. It was a miracle. Because I was given back the person I love most!

She asks if I want to text with her. God, yes! And we chatted for about 15 minutes. It was definitely her. We have insider jokes and ways of talking that can't be replicated. It felt like she had been resurrected. It brought tears to my eyes.

I knew that this was a gift that I shouldn't take for granted. Who knows how long it will last. So I made a point of telling her everything I wanted to tell her but couldn't all these past months. "I think of you every day." "I love you very much." "You are my favorite person in the world." "I've always been very grateful to have you in my life."

And what really, really got to me was that she told me she was proud of me. That's a huge deal. At seminal moments in the 24 years since my mother passed away, I've often wondered if she would be proud of me, and of course there's no way to know. So hearing that from Aunt Betty, the next best thing to a mother, meant everything to me.

They will be moving her to a less intensive part of the hospital soon, and hopefully she'll then have a phone in her room. But in the meantime, my sister and I sent her flowers. I figured she could use some color to offset all that New England snow. I'll also be sending her some photographs.

But I'm still in shock. Things like this just don't happen. A dear friend of mine would call it a mitzvah. All I know is I'm beyond grateful that I had the opportunity to say all those things that I needed to say to her. Because of that, whatever happens now, I'll be at peace.

And this profound life lesson got me thinking. Technically I have that gift with everyone I love. They're still here. But they won't always be. I should make the effort to tell everyone what I need to tell them as if it's their last day on earth.

Actually I've always known that on some level, but I take people for granted. It's a bad habit that many of us have. So I decided to invent a holiday for myself. I'm calling it Last Day. I'm going to celebrate it on the last day of every month, because that will be easy to remember, until such time as it becomes such a habit that I don't need to designate a special day.

On Last Day, I'm going to make an effort to tell people I love just how much they mean to me. I'm going to do it until they're sick of hearing it. I'm going to talk to these people as if this is our last day together, ever. Because some day, inevitably, it will be. But this is not meant to be a depressing holiday. Not at all. It's a celebration, because I've been given the gift of knowing how important these conversations are.

May I never forget.

Happy Last Day, dear reader, and thank you for making this blog so special.

First published on <u>*February 28, 2015*</u>

Dear Reader,

Thank you.

If you enjoyed this anthology, please tell your friends. ☺

It'll help keep my dogs in kibble!

~Barb

Meet the Author

So, exactly WHO is this woman and how does she do what she does?

Barb Abelhauser has been a bridgetender since 2001. She has opened 9 different drawbridges in 3 different states. To the best of her knowledge, other than her fellow bridgetender Dave (who has opened 11 bridges in 3 states), Barb is a record holder.

The opportunity to observe life from one very special, fixed point inspires her to write daily on her blog, The View from a Drawbridge."

Back in 2009, before she migrated to Seattle, she stepped into a StoryCorps booth that had parked itself in Jacksonville, Florida. That day she did an interview about her love of bridgetending. Then to her surprise, in 2015 she got a phone call. Part of the transcribed interview was to be included in the 2016 anthology entitled *Callings: The Purpose and Passion of Work*.

StoryCorps had chosen 53 stories out of 70,000 archived audio recordings; and hers was to be one of them. She felt honored.

Barb appreciates StoryCorps for inspiring her to start her blog and tell the stories of her inner and outer life. To express her ongoing gratitude, 10% of royalties from this book will be donated to StoryCorps.

She's been showcased on Storycorps, NPR's Morning Edition, Parade Magazine, Shaping Sapiens podcast, and in the September 2016 issue of O Magazine.

All of this unexpected and exciting attention has given her the courage to create a series of anthologies from her daily blog.

Barb has learned much from the years of being a bridgetender.

And, after a day of opening the drawbridge for a variety of vessels, she unwinds by capturing all those random thoughts and images of life unfolding that she witnessed while performing the many tasks required of her.

Since December 1, 2012 she has been publishing her musings 7 days a week--over 1380 posts that reveal what inspires her and what she cares about.

Her blogs are read by hundreds of loyal readers and those who comment make her day! In fact, it was on July 4, 2016 that she had her 100,000th visitor!

She truly believes that wisdom can be gained from daily life experience and observations that occur all around us, if only we take the time to watch and listen.

Born in Connecticut and raised in Florida, Barb now lives in Seattle, Washington with her two dogs. She writes and opens drawbridges every day.

About the Photographer

Amy Sassenberg has been interested in photography since childhood. Her photos reflect her joy in living and her enthusiastic nature. She currently has 50,000 pictures on her iPhone. She lives in Carnation, Washington, and was the first friend that Barb made upon moving to Seattle. All photos in this book were taken by Amy, with the exception of the image on page 33.

Whom We Appreciate

Shaping Sapiens—This website was created by my dear friend Amelia Isabel Torres. If you enjoy listening to podcasts, you'll find an interesting one here!
http://www.shapingsapiens.com/

Fresh Ground Stories—This is a monthly storytelling group that meets monthly in Seattle's Capitol Hill district. If you live in the area, I strongly suggest that you check it out.
http://www.meetup.com/Fresh-Ground-Stories/

Roy Street Coffee & Tea—This is the amazing coffee shop where Fresh Ground Stories meets every month. It's a nice mellow place to relax with friends.
http://www.roystreetcoffee.com/

StoryCorps—This is the organization that started me down the road to publishing. Ten percent of the royalties from this book will be donated to them, but it would be wonderful if you would support them, too! *https://storycorps.org*

Callings: The Purpose and Passion of Work by Dave Isay. This is the anthology that started it all for me. You'll find my story on page 17 of the collection.
https://storycorps.org/books/callings-the-purpose-and-passion-of-work/

The Royal Room—A delightful little venue in Seattle to listen to local jazz musicians. *http://theroyalroomseattle.com/*

Leah Tussing—A gifted vocalist who is well worth listening to, every chance you get.
https://www.reverbnation.com/leahtussing

Kiva.org—So far I've given 62 microloans to people in 52 different countries through this amazing organization. Won't you join me? *http://kiva.org*

National Public Radio—A great source of inspiration for my blog, and an even greater source of information for the wider world. *http://npr.org*

Arlo Guthrie—My all-time favorite folk singer and a purveyor of much wisdom. *http://www.arlo.net/*

Operation Sack Lunch—This little organization manages to provide nearly 436,000 free meals to Seattleites every year, and is worthy of your support. *http://www.oslserves.org/*

Authentic Writing Provokes—Learn more about my editor, and self-publishing specialist, Deborah Drake and enjoy her insights on writing. *http://authenticwritingprovokes.com*

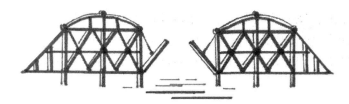

Made in the USA
Lexington, KY
16 September 2016